NONFICTION THAT SELLS:

YOUR GUIDE TO WRITING SUCCESS

BOOK IV IN THE SUCCESSFUL SELF-PUBLISHER SERIES

RAE A. STONEHOUSE

LIVE FOR EXCELLENCE PRODUCTIONS

ISBN - E-book: 978-1-998813-40-7

ISBN – Paperback: 978-1-998813-41-4

ISBN – Audiobook: 978-1-998813-42-1

INTRODUCTION TO BOOK FOUR IN THE SUCCESSFUL SELF-PUBLISHER SERIES

Welcome to Book Four in the Successful Self-Publisher Series: **Nonfiction That Sells: Your Guide to Writing Success.** Get ready to dive into a world filled with endless possibilities and triumphs!

After wrapping up the first three books in this exciting series, I felt like we'd covered all the bases. But then, a fresh question came my way from a client: "What's the magic ingredient that makes a nonfiction book a hit?" What a fantastic question to ponder!

The secret to making a nonfiction book a bestseller isn't just about having celebrity status or notoriety, but it's about touching people's hearts, communicating something genuine, and significant. This book will guide you through the intricate process of nonfiction writing, unveiling its complexities, and teaching you how to make your work accessible to the public.

You are about to embark on a journey of authenticity, discovery, and personal voice development. As we dive into this venture, remember that nonfiction writing is more than stating facts. It's about resonance, evoking emotions, and offering a fresh perspective.

This journey goes beyond writing; it's about establishing a connection, creating an impact, and leaving an indelible imprint. You're not just an author as you progress through this book; you are a guide, a teacher, and a storyteller, capable of creating a piece that's truthful, impactful, and representative of your unique voice.

Remember, writing is more than a skill—it's a means of touching people's hearts. Embrace this journey with both hands, and you will undoubtedly find the aptitude within you to create compelling nonfiction. Make it authentic, make it truthful, and make it uniquely yours.

This book is all about showing you the way to success. Each chapter builds on the last, offering fresh insights and new skills. It's designed to be a journey, so buckle up and read it from start to finish the first time. Later, come back to it and find the parts that speak to you the most.

As in my previous books, some ideas might come back in different chapters, but each time with a new twist. That's how we grow – by looking at things from various angles.

I've learned heaps putting this book together, and I can't wait to share it all with you. Let's embark on this exciting adventure together. Who knows? Maybe next time, it'll be YOUR name shining on that bestseller list! Here's to your writing success!

Welcome, and happy writing!

Rae A. Stonehouse

August 2023

CHAPTER ONE

INTRODUCTION TO WRITING NONFICTION: UNDERSTANDING THE GENRE, ITS MARKET, & YOUR TARGET AUDIENCE

UNDERSTANDING NONFICTION WRITING: Looking at What Makes Nonfiction Different from Things Like Fiction and Poetry

Nonfiction writing refers to a genre that presents factual and real-life information. It encompasses works based on truth, evidence, and research, providing a window into reality rather than representing imaginary stories as found in fiction or evoking emotions through metaphors like poetry. Nonfiction writing encompasses various forms, including essays, biographies, memoirs, news articles, scientific reports, and academic papers, among others.

The fundamental feature of nonfiction writing is its basis in reality. It aims to inform and educate readers about real-world events, people, places, ideas, or concepts. Nonfiction writers conduct extensive research, relying on primary and secondary sources that offer reliable and verifiable information. This research-driven approach ensures accuracy, supports arguments with evidence, and lets readers gain a deeper understanding of a topic.

On the other hand, fiction writing is characterized by its imaginative and creative elements. Authors create fictional worlds, characters, and events that might be inspired by real-life experiences. In fiction, the primary intention is often to entertain, evoke emotions, or explore complex themes through storytelling.

While nonfiction revolves around facts, fiction uses elements of story-telling such as plot development, character arcs, and narrative techniques to engage readers. Fiction writers have the freedom to invent scenarios and characters, enabling them to explore unique perspectives or present thought-provoking ideas without being confined to real-world limitations.

Similarly, poetry distinguishes itself from nonfiction by emphasizing the aesthetics of language, along with evoking emotions and conveying deep meaning through metaphor, symbolism, and imagery. Poets use various techniques, such as rhyme, rhythm, and meter, to create musical and lyrical compositions. The purpose of poetry often extends beyond conveying information, focusing more on personal expression, highlighting emotions, or encapsulating complex ideas in a condensed form.

While both fiction and poetry may have elements of truth or be inspired by real-life experiences, their primary objective lies in artistic expression and the exploration of human experiences through creative means.

Nonfiction writing stands apart from other genres, such as fiction and poetry, through its commitment to truth and reliance on factual infor-mation. Nonfiction aims to inform, educate, and provide readers with an accurate understanding of real-world events, people, or ideas. Fiction, on the other hand, focuses on imaginative storytelling to enter-tain or explore themes, while poetry emphasizes aesthetics and emotional resonance through metaphor and language. Each genre offers its unique approach to engaging readers and enriching our understanding of the world.

DIGGING INTO THE NONFICTION MARKET: GETTING TO KNOW WHAT'S HOT AND WHAT'S NOT FOR NONFICTION BOOKS, LIKE THE BIG HITS AND SPECIAL LITTLE CORNERS OF THE MARKET

Nonfiction books have become increasingly popular in recent years, catering to diverse readers who seek knowledge, inspiration, and personal growth. In this section, we will explore the current market trends and demands for nonfiction books, focusing on popular subgenres and niche markets. Whether you are an aspiring writer, publisher, or book enthusiast, understanding the evolving landscape of the nonfiction market is essential for success.

I. Nonfiction Books: An Ever-Growing Market

A. Rise in popularity and sales of nonfiction books:

Over the past few years, the nonfiction book market has experienced an astonishing rise in both popularity and sales. This surge can be attributed to several factors that have influenced readers to seek factual and informative literature.

One of the major factors contributing to the rise in popularity of nonfiction books is the growing interest in personal development and self-improvement. As people become more concerned about their mental well-being and want to enhance their skills or knowledge, they turn to nonfiction books that offer valuable insights and practical advice. Titles in this genre cover a wide range of topics such as psychology, personal finance, health and wellness, and success strategies. Readers are drawn to these books as they offer actionable steps and methodologies to improve their lives.

Additionally, the rise in popularity of podcasts and documentaries has played a significant role in boosting nonfiction book sales. Many individuals discover fascinating stories or intriguing ideas through these mediums, and they often turn to books to delve deeper into the topic.

Nonfiction books provide a more comprehensive exploration of the topics, offering readers a chance to explore the ideas and narratives in greater detail.

The current cultural climate has sparked a growing interest in nonfiction books focused on social issues and historical events. Readers now actively seek books that shed light on marginalized voices, untold stories, and alternative perspectives. As societal movements gain momentum, readers want to educate themselves and gain a better understanding of the world around them, making nonfiction books an invaluable resource.

Technology has also played a crucial role in the rise of nonfiction book popularity. With the advent of e-readers and audiobooks, accessing nonfiction titles has become more convenient and portable. Readers can now easily carry an entire library of nonfiction books on their devices, letting them dive into different topics whenever they desire. This accessibility and convenience have undoubtedly contributed to the surge in sales and popularity.

The increase in book clubs and online reading communities has fueled interest in nonfiction books. These communities provide readers with a platform to discuss, share recommendations, and engage in thought-provoking conversations about nonfiction literature. The sense of camaraderie and intellectual stimulation found within these communities has encouraged more people to explore nonfiction books as a form of leisure and self-enrichment.

The rise in popularity and sales of nonfiction books can be attributed to the growing interest in personal development, the influence of podcasts and documentaries, the exploration of social issues, the convenience of technology, and the rise of book clubs and reading communities. With readers seeking knowledge, personal growth, and a better understanding of the world, nonfiction literature has emerged as a powerful medium to satiate these intellectual needs.

B. Factors contributing to the growth of the nonfiction market:

Several key factors have contributed to the growth of the nonfiction market in recent years. These factors include:

Increased interest in personal development: Nonfiction books related to personal development, self-help, and motivation have seen significant growth in recent years. With a greater emphasis on self-improvement and achieving success, readers are drawn to books that offer practical advice, guidance, and inspiration.

Rising demand for expert knowledge: Readers are increasingly seeking books that provide specialized knowledge and expertise in various fields. Nonfiction books that offer insights, strategies, and solutions in areas such as business, finance, health, science, and technology have become highly popular as people strive to gain a competitive edge and stay informed.

Accessibility of information: The growth of digital platforms, such as e-books and online publications, has made it easier for readers to access nonfiction books. Readers can now download and read books on their smartphones, tablets, or e-readers, making it more convenient and cost-effective to consume nonfiction content.

Expansion of niche markets: Nonfiction books have also seen growth due to the expansion of niche markets. Readers with specific interests or hobbies, such as cooking, gardening, fitness, or travel, can find a wide range of nonfiction books tailored to their interests. Publishers have catered to these niche markets by offering specialized content that appeals to specific target audiences.

Impact of social media and influencers: Social media platforms have played a significant role in promoting nonfiction books and authors. Influencers and thought leaders have leveraged their online presence to recommend and discuss nonfiction works, leading to increased visibility and sales. Online book clubs, newsletters, and podcasts have also emerged, providing platforms for discussions and recommendations focused on nonfiction books.

Change in reading habits: With the popularity of podcasts and audiobooks, many readers are now consuming nonfiction content in audio format. This growth in audiobooks has introduced a new way of experiencing nonfiction books, appealing to those who prefer to listen rather than read. This shift in reading habits has expanded the nonfiction market to include an audio audience.

Overall, factors such as a growing interest in personal development, increased demand for expert knowledge, the accessibility of information through digital platforms, the expansion of niche markets, the impact of social media and influencers, and changes in reading habits have all contributed to the growth of the nonfiction market. As readers continue to seek knowledge, inspiration, and practical advice, the nonfiction genre is likely to continue thriving.

C. Nonfiction books as a way for self-improvement and personal development

Nonfiction books have long been revered as a valuable tool for self-improvement and personal development. These books offer a wealth of knowledge and insights into various aspects of life, letting readers gain a deeper understanding of themselves and the world around them. Here, we explore why nonfiction books serve as an effective way for self-improvement and personal growth.

Practical Advice and Guidance: Nonfiction books often provide practical advice and guidance on a specific topic or skill. Whether it's managing one's finances, cultivating better relationships, or developing effective communication skills, these books offer step-by-step strategies and techniques that can be applied to real-life situations. By implementing the advice offered in these books, readers can make positive changes in their lives and move closer to their goals.

Broadening Perspectives: Nonfiction books also serve as a medium for broadening perspectives. They provide readers with diverse viewpoints and insights into various subjects, such as history, philosophy, science, or culture. By exposing themselves to different perspectives and ideas, readers can challenge their own beliefs, deepen their understanding of the world, and experience personal growth.

Mindset and Emotional Well-being: Many nonfiction books focus on mindset and emotional well-being. They delve into topics like mindfulness, resilience, happiness, and emotional intelligence, helping readers develop a healthier mindset and emotional toolkit. By learning to cultivate a positive mindset, manage stress, and regulate emotions, individuals can enhance their overall well-being, leading to increased self-improvement and personal growth.

Self-Reflection and Self-Awareness: Nonfiction books often encourage self-reflection, prompting readers to examine their thoughts, beliefs, and behaviors. By engaging in introspection and developing self-awareness, individuals can identify their strengths, weaknesses, and areas for improvement. This self-reflection is a catalyst for personal growth, as it enables individuals to make conscious choices and take actions that align with their values and goals.

Inspiring Role Models: Many nonfiction books feature real-life stories of successful individuals who have overcome challenges and achieved greatness. These inspiring role models serve as a source of motivation for readers, showing them that personal growth and success are within reach. By studying the journeys of these individuals, readers can gain insights into their mindset, habits, and strategies, which they can then apply in their own lives.

Nonfiction books are an invaluable resource for self-improvement and personal development. They offer practical advice, broaden perspectives, promote a healthier mindset, encourage self-reflection, and provide inspiring role models. By reading and implementing the wisdom shared in these books, individuals can embark on a journey of self-discovery, growth, and transformation.

II. Popular Subgenres in Nonfiction

A. Memoirs and Biographies: The fascination with real-life stories.

B. Self-help and Motivational Books: Catering to personal growth and empowerment.

C. History and Politics: Insights into our past and present.

D. Science and Popular Science: Making complex subjects accessible.

E. Business and Personal Finance: Practical advice for success.

F. True Crime and Investigative Journalism: Uncovering real-life mysteries.

G. Health and Wellness: The growing interest in physical and mental well-being.

III. Niche Markets and Emerging Trends

A. Environmental and Sustainability: Focus on climate change and conservation.

B. Personal Finance for Millennials: Addressing financial challenges for younger generations.

C. Mental Health and Mindfulness: Coping strategies and fostering well-being.

D. Diverse Voices: Representation and inclusiveness in nonfiction.

E. Social Justice and Activism: Inspiring change and promoting awareness.

F. Travel and Adventure Writing: Exploration and personal experiences.

G. Food and Culinary: The evolving world of gastronomy.

H. Technology and Futurism: Insights into the digital era and innovative advancements.

IV. Publishing and Marketing Strategies for Nonfiction Authors

A. Researching the target audience and identifying market gaps.

B. Building a strong author platform and online presence.

C. Collaborating with traditional publishers or choosing self-publishing.

D. Leveraging social media, blogging, and podcasting for book promotion.

E. Engaging with book clubs, libraries, and niche communities.

The nonfiction market offers a diverse array of subgenres and niche markets, making it a compelling space for writers and publishers. By understanding the current trends and demands, authors can tap into readers' interests and create compelling nonfiction books that resonate with their target audience. As the market continues to evolve, it is essential to stay up to date with emerging trends, engage with readers, and adapt publishing and marketing strategies. May this exploration of the nonfiction market empower you to find your niche and succeed in your nonfiction writing endeavors.

IDENTIFYING YOUR TARGET AUDIENCE: DOING YOUR HOMEWORK TO PINPOINT JUST WHO YOUR READERS MIGHT BE

Identifying your target audience is a crucial step when writing a nonfiction book. By understanding who your readers are, their interests, and their needs, you can tailor your content to meet their expectations and provide value. Conducting thorough research can help you gather the information to pinpoint your specific readership. Here are steps to consider:

Define the purpose of your book: Start by clarifying the purpose of your nonfiction book. What problem does it solve? What information does it provide? Understanding your book's goals will help you determine who would benefit the most from it.

Conduct market research: Begin by conducting market research to gain insights into your potential audience. Look for similar books in your niche and study their readership. Analyze reviews, comments, and social media discussions related to those books to understand what readers liked or disliked about them. This will provide a good starting point for identifying your target audience.

Consider demographics: Demographics play a significant role in understanding your readership. Factors such as age, gender, location, education level, and occupation can significantly influence their preferences and needs. Analyzing data from market research firms, social media platforms, or conducting surveys can provide valuable insights into the demographic composition of your target audience.

Study interests and preferences: Dive deeper into the interests and preferences of your potential readers. Look for online communities, forums, or social media groups related to your book's topic. Engage with these communities to understand what challenges, needs, or interests they are discussing. This can help you tailor your book to address those specific concerns and capture their attention.

Identify specific needs: Nonfiction books typically aim to fulfill a specific need or provide practical knowledge to readers. Identify the specific needs of your target audience related to your book's niche. This could address their pain points, offering solutions, or satisfying their intellectual curiosity. Focusing on these needs will make your book more appealing to your target audience.

Create reader personas: Once you have gathered enough information through research, create reader personas. These fictional profiles represent different segments of your target audience. Include details such as age, occupation, interests, challenges, and needs for each persona. These personas will help you gain a deeper understanding of your readers, enabling you to write with them in mind.

Test your assumptions: While your research and reader personas provide a solid foundation, it is essential to confirm your assumptions. Share your book concept with a small group of individuals representing your target audience and gather their feedback. Use their insights to refine your approach and make sure your book resonates with your readership.

Identifying your target audience is an ongoing process. As you continue to write and promote your book, collect feedback, engage with readers, and adapt to evolve your understanding of your audience. This will make sure your nonfiction book meets the needs and expectations of your specific readership.

MAKING YOUR WRITING FIT THE PEOPLE READING IT: FINDING A WAY TO WRITE THAT HITS HOME WITH THE PEOPLE YOU WANT TO REACH, MAKING SURE WHAT YOU WRITE GRABS THEM AND TALKS ABOUT STUFF THEY CARE ABOUT

When it comes to effective communication, understanding your audience is key. Whether you are writing a blog post, an email, or marketing copy, tailoring your writing to resonate with your target audience is crucial. In this guide, we will explore how to develop a writing style, tone, and structure that will engage and interest your readers.

Define your target audience: The first step in tailoring your writing is to clearly identify your target audience. Consider their demographics, interests, and goals. Are they professionals, students, or hobbyists? What level of knowledge do they have? Understanding your audience will help you craft a message that is specific and relevant.

Use appropriate language: Once you know who you are writing for, adapt your language accordingly. Avoid using jargon or technical terms that might confuse your audience. Instead, choose clear and concise language that your readers will understand. However, if your audience consists of experts or professionals, you may need to use specialized language to cater to their needs.

Establish a tone: Your writing tone refers to the overall mood or attitude you convey through your words. Consider the emotions and feelings you want to evoke in your audience. Are you aiming for a formal and professional tone, or a more casual and friendly one? Your tone should align with both your content and your audience's preferences.

Structure your content: Developing a coherent structure helps your audience navigate your writing effectively. Begin with a compelling introduction that grabs their attention and clearly states the purpose of your piece. In the body, organize your content into logical sections or subheadings. Use bullet points or numbered lists to break down complex information and make it more digestible. Finally, end with a strong conclusion that summarizes key points and encourages action or further reading.

Maintain engagement: To keep your audience engaged throughout your piece, consider incorporating storytelling, anecdotes, or relevant examples. Use descriptive language to paint vivid pictures and create mental images. Vary sentence length and structure to add rhythm and flow to your writing. Additionally, consider using visual aids such as images, infographics, or data charts, if appropriate, to enhance comprehension and engagement.

Personalize your content: Show your audience that you understand their needs and interests by personalizing your content. Address their pain points, desires, or challenges relevant to your topic. Use inclusive language and speak directly to your readers, using words like "you" and "we." This helps build a connection and makes your writing more relatable.

Test and refine: Once you have crafted your writing for your target audience, it's essential to test the effectiveness of your content. Track engagement metrics such as read time, clicks, and comments to gauge how well your writing resonates with your audience. Analyze feedback and make necessary adjustments to continuously refine your writing style.

By tailoring your writing style, tone, and structure to your target audience, you can create content engaging, relevant, and resonates with their interests. Remember to continuously test and adapt your approach based on feedback and analytics to ensure your writing remains effective and impactful.

UNDERSTANDING THE IMPORTANCE OF AUTHENTICITY: THE SIGNIFICANCE OF CREDIBILITY & ACCURACY IN NONFICTION WRITING

In the realm of nonfiction writing, authenticity serves as the cornerstone on which credibility and accuracy are built. Whether crafting an article, essay, or any piece of prose grounded in reality, writers must focus on thorough research, fact-checking, and citing reliable sources. By doing so, they can ensure their work is trustworthy, informative, and impactful.

Proper research lies at the foundation of nonfiction writing. It involves a comprehensive examination of the topic at hand, delving into various primary and secondary sources. Investing time and effort into gathering relevant information lets writers present a well-rounded perspective, thus strengthening the credibility of their work. The deeper the dive into research, the more nuanced and compelling the final piece can become.

Fact-checking is an essential step in the writing process that verifies the accuracy of information. As nonfiction writers, one must strive to provide readers with an accurate representation of reality. By meticulously cross-referencing facts, statistics, and claims, writers safeguard against the dissemination of misinformation and uphold the integrity of their work. Fact-checking acts as a protective shield against inadvertent errors or deliberate manipulation, making sure readers can rely on the information.

Citing reliable sources bolsters the transparency and credibility of nonfiction writing. Using diverse sources, such as peer-reviewed journals, reputable news outlets, and renowned experts, lends weight and authority to the arguments. Additionally, citing sources lets readers continue their own exploration and evaluation of the topic, promoting intellectual growth and fostering an engaged and informed readership. Providing proper citations shows the writer acknowledges the contributions of others and values the collective knowledge that enriches their work.

In today's information age, where the line between fact and fiction can blur, the importance of authenticity in nonfiction writing cannot be overstated. Misinformation can have far-reaching consequences, shaping public opinion and decision-making. By adhering to a rigorous process of thorough research, fact-checking, and citing reliable sources, nonfiction writers can stand as beacons of truth, counteracting the spread of falsehoods and disinformation.

Authenticity lets writers establish themselves as trusted voices in their respective fields. Readers seek authors who focus on accuracy, credibility, and transparency, turning to them as reliable sources of information. This trust can have a lasting impact, fostering a loyal readership and opening doors to further opportunities for writers to create positive change and influence public discourse.

Authenticity serves as the bedrock of nonfiction writing, ensuring credibility and accuracy. Thorough research, fact-checking, and citing reliable sources are essential parts that are the foundation on which impactful and trustworthy nonfiction work is built. By focusing on authenticity, writers can contribute to a healthier, more informed, and critically thinking society.

FINDING YOUR WAY THROUGH THE RIGHT AND WRONG STUFF: NAVIGATING ETHICAL CONSIDERATIONS

Navigating ethical considerations:

Discussing ethical responsibilities as a nonfiction writer, including avoiding plagiarism, respecting privacy, and maintaining transparency with readers.

As a nonfiction writer, it is imperative to have a strong understanding of ethical responsibilities. When crafting content that presents factual information, writers must strive to ensure accuracy, maintain integrity, and uphold the trust of their readers. There are three key ethical considerations to navigate: avoiding plagiarism, respecting privacy, and maintaining transparency.

Avoiding plagiarism is an essential ethical responsibility that nonfiction writers must take seriously. Plagiarism involves presenting someone else's work, ideas, or words as your own without giving proper credit. This unethical practice undermines credibility and intellectual integrity. To prevent plagiarism, it is crucial to always attribute and cite sources accurately. Clearly indicate quotes, paraphrases, and references, citing the original author or source. By doing so, writers respect others' intellectual property while upholding professional standards.

Another important ethical aspect is respecting privacy when writing nonfiction. It is essential to consider the potential impact of revealing personal or private information without consent. This pertains not only to individuals but also to corporations, organizations, or communities. Writers should obtain permission when sharing personal stories, interviews, or sensitive information that could potentially harm someone's reputation or invade their privacy. Respecting boundaries fosters trust and ensures ethical conduct, setting a strong foundation for nonfiction writing.

Maintaining transparency with readers is the backbone of ethical nonfiction writing. Writers have a responsibility to disclose their affiliations, financial interests, or any potential biases that may influence their work. By remaining transparent, readers can make more informed judgments about the information presented to them. Transparency also lets readers evaluate the credibility and potential conflicts of interest. Nonfiction writers should clearly identify any potential biases or vested interests that may affect the accuracy or objectivity of the information they present.

Additionally, maintaining transparency also means accurately representing the scope and limitations of the research or evidence presented. Writers should avoid exaggeration or misrepresentation that could mislead readers. By providing contextual information, acknowledging uncertainties, and being honest about the limits of knowledge, writers make sure readers clearly understand the topic being discussed.

Nonfiction writers bear ethical responsibilities that encompass avoiding plagiarism, respecting privacy, and maintaining transparency. By accurately attributing sources, seeking consent when sharing personal information, and being transparent about affiliations or biases, writers can uphold their integrity, earn trust, and produce content that is both credible and ethical. Striving to navigate these ethical considerations is not only essential for individual writers but also for the overall credibility and trustworthiness of the nonfiction genre.

EMBRACING THE NONFICTION WRITING JOURNEY:

Encouraging writers to embrace the challenges and rewards of writing nonfiction, highlighting the potential impact of their work in educating, inspiring, or informing their readers.

In a world often dominated by fictional narratives, nonfiction writing stands as a powerful medium to educate, inspire, and inform readers. While the path of nonfiction writing may be fraught with challenges, writers must embrace this journey, for the rewards can be transformative.

One of the key aspects of the nonfiction writing journey is the pursuit of knowledge and understanding. Writers delve into a vast array of topics, mining facts and exploring their depths in search of universal truths. Each nonfiction writer becomes a lifelong student, driven by a thirst for knowledge and a desire to share their discoveries with the world. By embarking on such a journey, writers invite readers to join them in their exploration of the intricacies of the human experience and the wonders and mysteries of the world we inhabit.

While pursuing knowledge fuels the nonfiction writing journey, the potential for impact should not be overlooked. Nonfiction writing has the unique ability to educate and inform readers, enabling them to gain a deeper understanding of various subjects. Through well-researched arguments and balanced perspectives, writers can challenge prevailing beliefs, broaden horizons, and present new ways of thinking. By embracing the power of nonfiction writing, writers can become catalysts for change, guiding readers toward alternative viewpoints and inspiring them to question long-held assumptions.

Nonfiction writing has the potential to inspire and ignite a spark within readers. By sharing stories of triumph, resilience, and personal growth, writers can cultivate empathy, foster connections, and give a voice to those who have been silenced. Nonfiction narratives reveal the extraordinary within the ordinary, showing readers that real-life experiences can be as captivating and transformative as the tales spun by fiction. By embracing the emotional part of nonfiction writing, writers can leave an indelible imprint on readers' lives, empowering them to find their own paths and create their own narratives.

However, the nonfiction writing journey comes with its fair share of challenges. Researching complex topics, verifying sources, and maintaining objectivity can require immense dedication and perseverance. Writers must be willing to navigate through the countless sources of information, sifting through contradictory narratives, and discerning between reliable and unreliable sources. The craft of storytelling within nonfiction writing demands precision, as writers strive to create narratives that engage and captivate readers while staying faithful to factual accuracy. Embracing these challenges is crucial for honing the skills necessary to make a lasting impact.

Ultimately, the journey of nonfiction writing allows writers to inform, inspire, and educate. It is a path that requires resilience, curiosity, and a commitment to truth and accuracy. By embracing the challenges and rewards of nonfiction writing, writers can contribute to a more informed and empathetic society. Whether educating readers about historical events, sharing personal struggles and triumphs, or shedding light on societal issues, nonfiction writers have the power to shape the hearts and minds of readers and reshape the world.

Chapter Summary:

Chapter 1 is all about the world of nonfiction writing. Here's what you need to know:

Understanding Nonfiction Writing: It's not like fiction or poetry. Nonfiction is about truth and real-life stuff. It comes in many forms like essays, reports, biographies, and more.

Digging into the Nonfiction Market: Nonfiction books are getting more popular. Subjects like self-help, social issues, and personal development are hot. Technology and changes in how people read are boosting sales.

Identifying Your Target Audience: You've got to know who's going to read your book. Think about what they want and need, do your research, and keep learning about them.

Making Your Writing Fit the People Reading It: Keep it simple and clear. Know your readers and write in a way they'll connect with.

Understanding Authenticity: Spend time researching and checking facts. Keep it real and true.

Navigating Ethical Considerations: Be honest, fair, and respectful. Don't steal ideas and be careful with private information.

Briefly, writing nonfiction is about knowing your readers, finding the truth, and sharing it in a way that's clear and fair. It's hard work, but it can change lives and even the world. It's about showing people the real magic in everyday life and inspiring them to create their own stories.

In our Next Chapter...

Get ready for Chapter 2! Are you ready to craft a book that goes beyond mere words on a page? We're about to delve into the heart of bringing your book to life.

First things first, we'll uncover that perfect topic. Something you're passionate about, something that ignites your spirit, and something that will compel readers to spread the word: "This is a must-read!" Next, we'll dive into the depths of your being.

Next, we'll dig into YOU. Yep, your strengths, your loves, your life – all that stuff is going to make your writing sizzle.

But let's not forget about our readers. We'll delve into their minds and hearts, understanding what makes them tick.

We'll uncover the trends, anticipate what's coming next, and learn how to connect with them like an old friend. And that's not all!

We'll equip you with some fantastic tools and invaluable tips to blend your passions with profitability.

We'll brainstorm those million-dollar ideas and even show you how to seek feedback from trusted individuals.

So, buckle up, grab your pen, and prepare to plunge into Chapter 2. It's not just about writing; it's about discovering that special something that will make your book a sensation. It's as simple as that! See you in Chapter 2!

CHAPTER TWO

CHOOSING THE RIGHT TOPIC: IDENTIFYING YOUR UNIQUE AREA OF EXPERTISE OR PASSION AND FINDING A SUBJECT THAT RESONATES WITH READERS

WHY PICKING THE RIGHT TOPIC MATTERS:

EXPLORING the significance of selecting a topic that aligns with your knowledge or passion and resonates with readers to ensure a compelling and engaging book.

Choosing the right topic for a book is a critical decision, as it lays the foundation for the entire work. A well-chosen topic can ignite the author's passion and let their expertise shine, while also captivating readers and ensuring their engagement throughout the book. This chapter delves into the significance of selecting a topic that aligns with an author's knowledge or passion and resonates with readers, emphasizing how it can contribute to the creation of a compelling and engaging book.

Establishing a Personal Connection:

Choosing a topic that aligns with an author's knowledge or passion establishes a strong personal connection between the author and the book. It lets the author draw upon their knowledge, experience, and enthusiasm, infusing the writing with authenticity and depth. When an author cares about the topic, their passion shines through, making the book more compelling for readers.

Leveraging Expertise:

Selecting a topic that aligns with an author's expertise lets them leverage their unique knowledge and insights, ultimately enhancing the quality of their writing. An author who has a deep understanding of the topic can provide valuable and reliable information, creating a sense of credibility and trustworthiness among readers. Knowledge can also help the author effectively communicate complex ideas, making the book accessible and engaging for readers of various levels of familiarity with the topic.

Captivating Readers:

Choosing a topic that resonates with readers is crucial for capturing their attention and keeping them engaged. An author must consider their target audience and select a topic that aligns with their interests, concerns, or aspirations. By addressing issues that readers care about, the book becomes more relatable, inspiring readers to connect with the content on a personal level. When readers find the topic relevant and compelling, they are more likely to invest time and energy in the book, driving its overall success.

Fostering Emotional Connection:

A well-chosen topic has the power to evoke emotions in readers, leaving a lasting impact on their minds and hearts. Whether it is a thought-provoking idea, an inspiring story, or a challenging perspective, selecting a topic that resonates emotionally with readers lets the book make a deeper affect. Emotionally engaged readers are more likely to recommend the book to others, spread positive word-of-mouth, and become avid supporters of the author's work.

Selecting the right topic for a book is a pivotal part of the writing process. By choosing a subject that aligns with an author's knowledge or passion and resonates with readers, an author can craft a compelling and engaging book. Through personal connection, leveraging knowledge, captivating readers, and fostering emotional engagement, a well-chosen topic can elevate the overall quality and success of the book. Authors should take the time to carefully consider their options, making sure their chosen topic will ignite their passion, resonate with readers, and create a lasting impact.

Taking a Good Look at What You Know Best:

Assessing your personal strengths, experiences, and knowledge is an essential step in identifying your unique area of knowledge and the subjects you can authentically write about. Evaluating your knowledge enables you to contribute valuable and meaningful content to your readers or audience. Here is a step-by-step guide to help you in this process:

Identify your strengths: Think about the skills, talents, and attributes that set you apart from others. Consider your professional experience, hobbies, or any specialized knowledge you have. These strengths can be broad, such as excellent communication skills or specific, like knowledge in a particular software or field.

Reflect on your experiences: Consider the experiences you have had throughout your life. Think about your education, career, personal projects, or volunteer work. Look for common threads or recurring themes in these experiences. Pay attention to what you have learned, achieved, or overcome.

Determine your knowledge base: Analyze your depth of knowledge in specific subjects or fields. Ask yourself questions like: What topics do you have extensive knowledge about? What subjects do people often seek your advice on? Where do you naturally gravitate when engaging in conversations or conducting research?

Consider your passions and interests: Identify the topics you genuinely enjoy exploring and learning about. Consider what keeps you engaged and motivated. Passion for a subject is essential as it will fuel your desire to continually expand your knowledge and share your insights.

Narrow down your focus: After completing the previous steps, you should have a general idea of your area of knowledge. However, it's essential to further refine your focus to make your knowledge more distinctive. Consider if there is a specific niche or subfield within your broader area where you can specialize. Narrowing down your focus will not only distinguish you but also position you as an authoritative voice in that specific area.

Confirm your knowledge: Once you have identified your area of knowledge, it is crucial to validate it objectively. Seek feedback from trusted colleagues, mentors, or experts in your field. Engage in conversations, join relevant professional networks, or go to conferences to gauge your knowledge level and gather insights from others. This validation will help you gain confidence in your knowledge and identify areas for improvement.

Note audience needs: last, consider the audience you want to reach. Assess their needs, pain points, and the content they typically consume. Align your knowledge with their requirements to ensure your writing will resonate with them and provide value.

By following these steps, you can assess your personal strengths, experiences, and knowledge effectively. Identifying your unique area of knowledge will let you authentically write about subjects that resonate with you and offer valuable insights to your audience. Remember, continuous learning and growth are essential to staying relevant and expanding your knowledge.

Digging into What Readers Want: Looking into the Market to Find Out What People Like to Read and Spotting Subjects or Trends That Are Big Now or Could Be a Big Deal Down the Road.

Market research is a crucial step in determining the demand and preferences of readers. By investigating the market, identifying current popular subjects or trends, and expecting potential future trends, authors and publishers can align their content with what readers want. Here are three key aspects to consider when researching market demand:

Analyzing current popular subjects/trends:

A comprehensive analysis of current popular subjects or trends lets authors and publishers effectively meet the demands of the market. This can be done by examining bestseller lists, book reviews, blog posts, social media discussions, and other sources highlighting readers' preferences. By studying the success of similar books or content in specific genres, authors can identify what topics or themes resonate with their target audience.

For example, if psychological thrillers are currently popular, research can reveal the elements that make them appeal - such as complex characters, intricate plot twists, or unique settings. Authors and publishers can then incorporate these elements into their own work, creating content that aligns with the current trends and piques the readers' interest.

Identifying emerging trends:

In addition to studying current popular subjects, it is crucial to be aware of emerging trends. Identifying subjects or themes gaining traction can provide authors and publishers with the opportunity to capitalize on future demand. Following industry news, attending book fairs or conferences, networking with other authors, and engaging with online communities can provide insights into emerging trends.

For example, if there is a growing interest in sustainability and eco-friendly practices, authors might consider exploring topics like green living, climate change, or sustainable fashion as potential subjects for their next book. Jumping ahead of the curve and recognizing these emerging trends can help authors remain innovative and relevant to the market.

Gathering reader feedback:

Directly engaging with readers through surveys, focus groups, or online platforms can offer valuable insights into their preferences. Conducting surveys to assess readers' interests, analyzing reviews, and tracking feedback on social media can help authors understand what readers like, dislike, and desire in their reading experiences.

For example, if a survey reveals that readers are seeking diverse representation in young adult literature, authors can focus on developing stories that encompass a wide range of characters from various backgrounds. By gathering feedback and addressing readers' preferences, authors can build a loyal fanbase and create content that resonates with a broader audience.

Researching market demand involves investigating readers' preferences, identifying current popular subjects or trends, and expecting future trends. By analyzing the market, authors and publishers can tailor their content to meet the demands of readers, increase their visibility, and maintain relevance in a rapidly changing publishing landscape.

HITTING THE RIGHT NOTE WITH READERS: GETTING WHAT THE PEOPLE YOU WANT TO REACH ARE INTO, WHAT THEY EXPECT, AND WHAT THEY NEED, SO YOU CAN PICK A TOPIC THAT REALLY TALKS TO THEM AND MAKES A CONNECTION THAT KEEPS THEM HOOKED.

Finding resonance with readers is an essential part of successful writing. It involves understanding the interests, expectations, and needs of the target audience to choose a topic that resonates deeply with them. By doing so, a writer can establish a strong connection with their readers and foster engagement. Here are key strategies to meet this goal:

Conduct thorough audience research: Start by identifying your target audience. Analyze their demographics such as age, gender, education, and location. This will help you understand their general interests and preferences. Follow this up by conducting surveys, interviews, or focus groups to dig deeper into their specific needs and expectations.

Explore trending topics and themes: Stay updated with the latest trends and hot topics relevant to your niche. Track social media platforms, online forums, and news sites to gauge what is capturing the attention of your target audience. Look for common threads or recurring themes that can be developed into engaging topics.

Identify pain points and challenges: Consider the challenges or problems your target audience may face within your niche. Address these pain points directly, offering solutions, advice, or inspirational stories that can resonate deeply with readers. This establishes a connection by showing empathy and understanding their needs.

Analyze successful content within your niche: Study popular blogs, articles, or books that have resonated with your target audience. Look for patterns in the content, writing style, and themes that made those pieces successful. Adapt those learnings to create your unique content, ensuring it aligns with your readers' interests and expectations.

Use storytelling techniques: Humans are wired to respond to stories. Craft your content by weaving stories or personal anecdotes that relate to your topic. Emotionally engaging narratives can capture your readers' attention and make your content more relatable. This connection enhances resonance and creates a memorable experience for your audience.

Use inclusive and conversational language: Tailor your writing style to match your target audience's preferences. Use language that is accessible, conversational, and inclusive. Avoid jargon or overly formal language unless your audience demands it. By speaking directly to your readers in a relatable tone, you create a sense of connection that fosters engagement.

Seek feedback and engage with your audience: Actively seek feedback from your readers through comments, emails, or social media platforms. Engage in conversations with them, ask for their opinions, and respond to their queries. This interaction not only helps you understand their needs better but also builds a sense of community and loyalty.

Remember that finding resonance requires continuous effort and adaptation. Keep track of what works and what doesn't by analyzing engagement metrics such as views, shares, comments, and conversions. Tailor your future content to align with the interests and needs of your audience, evolving along with their preferences. By consistently striving to understand and connect with your readers, you can build a strong and engaged audience base.

MIXING WHAT YOU LOVE WITH WHAT CAN MAKE MONEY:

In today's competitive landscape, deciding on a topic to pursue can be a challenging task. On one hand, our passions drive us to explore areas we are interested in and connected to. But considering the market potential and profitability of that topic is essential for ensuring long-term success and sustainability. So balancing passion and profitability becomes crucial in topic choice.

Passion is the fuel that propels us forward. When we are passionate about a subject, we dive deep into its intricacies and feel a strong sense of fulfillment. It keeps us motivated through highs and lows, enabling us to withstand obstacles and setbacks. Pursuing a topic, we are passionate about brings an inherent joy to our work and lets us bring our best selves to it. This enthusiasm and dedication often translate into quality outputs, helping us stand out in a crowded marketplace.

However, while passion is important, it may not always guarantee success from a financial perspective. Market potential and profitability should not be overlooked, as they ultimately sustain our ventures. Conducting thorough research to evaluate the viability of a topic can provide valuable insights into its demand, competition, and revenue potential. Analyzing market trends, consumer needs, and competition can help identify gaps or niches to be filled. By balancing passion with market analysis, we increase the chances of selecting a topic that not only resonates with us but also has the potential to generate revenue and attract customers.

A well-rounded approach to topic selection involves assessing our personal interests alongside objective data to make an informed decision. This process may require evaluating multiple ideas, conducting feasibility studies, and seeking external perspectives. It is essential to ask ourselves critical questions such as: Are there existing products or services related to our topic? What is the target audience's willingness to pay? Are there any foreseeable challenges or risks? This careful evaluation makes sure our passions align with real-world opportunities, reducing the chances of investing our time and resources in a topic that may not yield returns.

A good balance between passion and profitability can provide a sustainable advantage eventually. By selecting a topic that we are passionate about, we are more likely to invest the time and effort required to improve and refine our offerings continuously. The genuine commitment that arises from passion lets us establish ourselves as experts, build a loyal customer base, and innovate in our chosen field. Simultaneously, profitability makes sure our endeavors are economically viable, enabling us to reinvest in growth, expand our reach, and explore new opportunities.

Finding the right balance between passion and profitability is essential when selecting a topic to pursue. Passion fuels our drive and helps us achieve excellence, while profitability ensures our venture's sustainability. Weighing the importance of pursuing a topic we are passionate about with considering its market potential offers a well-rounded approach to topic selection. By striking this balance, we increase the likelihood of success, fulfillment, and continued growth in our chosen field.

BRAINSTORMING AND REFINING IDEAS:

Brainstorming and refining ideas is a crucial step in the creative process. It involves generating a wide range of ideas and then selecting and refining the most promising ones. Various techniques can facilitate this process, such as mind mapping, journaling, or discussion groups. Each technique offers a unique approach to idea generation and refinement. Here's a breakdown of these techniques:

Mind Mapping: Mind mapping is a visual tool that helps organize thoughts and ideas. Start with a central topic or theme, and then branch out with related ideas. This technique allows for free-flowing ideas and encourages non-linear thinking. As you brainstorm various ideas, you can make connections and identify the core essence of the topic.

Journaling: Journaling involves writing down thoughts, ideas, and observations. It provides a way to reflect on different parts of the topic and explore potential angles. Through consistent journaling, you can generate a plethora of ideas and insights. Reviewing and analyzing these entries will help you identify and refine the essence of the topic.

Discussion Groups: Engaging with others through discussion groups can be a valuable technique for idea generation. When different perspectives are involved, it enhances the brainstorming process. Group members can bounce ideas off each other, provide feedback, and challenge assumptions. By discussing and debating, you can collectively refine the topic's core essence.

The combination of these techniques allows for a diverse range of ideas to be generated and explored. Once you have an extensive list of ideas, it's time to narrow them down and refine the topic to its core essence. Here are a few strategies for this refining stage:

Identify common threads: Look for recurring themes, patterns, or connections among the ideas. These common threads can help you identify the essential parts of the topic.

Prioritize ideas: Evaluate each idea based on its relevance, feasibility, uniqueness, and potential impact. By ranking the ideas, you can determine which ones hold the most promise and align with the core essence you seek.

Seek feedback: Share your ideas with others and gather feedback. This outside perspective can help you gain insights and confirm your understanding of the topic's core essence.

Reframe and redefine: Consider reframing the topic or redefining its scope to make sure it aligns with the refined essence. Look for ways to make it more specific, impactful, or focused.

Using these brainstorming and refining techniques, you can generate a multitude of ideas and gradually narrow them down to the core essence of the topic. These processes encourage creativity, foster collaboration, and make sure you uncover the most valuable and meaningful ideas.

SEEKING FEEDBACK AND VALIDATION FOR POTENTIAL TOPIC IDEAS:

Dear [Name],

I hope this message finds you well! I am contacting you as one of the trusted individuals in my network, seeking your feedback and validation on potential topic ideas for an upcoming project. Your insights and perspectives are invaluable, and I appreciate your time and knowledge.

As I embark on this creative journey, I must select a topic that will captivate and resonate with a wide readership. To ensure its success, I believe it is important to gather feedback and validation from those I trust. Your honest input will not only help me identify the most engaging subject matter, but it will also provide me with a valuable perspective I may have overlooked.

Below are a few potential topic ideas I have been considering:

1. Exploring the impact of technology on interpersonal relationships and society.

2. Unveiling lesser-known personal stories and struggles of influential historical figures.

3. Investigating the role of environmental preservation in mitigating the effects of climate change.

4. Analyzing the portrayal of mental health in contemporary literature and media.

While these suggestions are by no means exhaustive, I believe they offer a strong starting point for discussion. I am open to any suggestions, alterations, or new ideas you think may have more potential to engage readers across various backgrounds.

I kindly ask you to consider these aspects when providing your feedback:

1. Relevance: How pertinent is the topic in today's world? Will it resonate with a wide range of readers?

2. Novelty: Is the topic fresh and innovative? Will it bring a new perspective to the table?

3. Depth: Does the topic offer multiple layers and avenues for exploration, allowing for a comprehensive analysis?

4. Appeal: Will this topic captivate the interest of readers and encourage them to delve deeper into the topic?

Please share your thoughts, suggestions, or concerns regarding the potential topics or other ideas you might have. Your feedback will greatly contribute to my decision-making process and help me refine my focus.

Thank you immensely for your time and consideration. Your support means the world and I look forward to hearing your valuable insights.

Warm regards,

[Your Name]

Chapter Summary:

Chapter 2 sets the foundation for your writing journey, divided into three essential parts.

First, we focus on selecting a proper topic. The aim here is to find a topic that resonates with you and interests the reader. Striking the right balance will naturally engage your audience.

The second part emphasizes introspection, urging you to tap into your unique experiences and knowledge. Your personal touch, combined with your passion and expertise, will add authenticity to your book, making it stand out.

Finally, we explore the art of understanding reader trends. Stay abreast with the latest preferences, expect future trends, and be open to reader input.

We recommend strategies for aligning your passion with potential profitability, offer tips for idea generation and refinement, and stress the importance of feedback. Chapter 2 essentially bridges the gap between self-awareness, reader insight, and finding the ideal blend to ensure your book's success. It's about simplicity and strategy.

In our Next Chapter...

Ready to delve into the fascinating world of research?

Look no further than Chapter 3!

Whether you're a novice or a seasoned expert, this chapter simplifies the research process into easily understandable steps.

Begin by formulating SMART questions that guide your study. Uncover missing elements by reviewing past work. From selecting the perfect design to gathering and analyzing data, this chapter covers it all. You'll even receive guidance on ethical considerations to ensure you navigate with care.

Concerned about the reliability of your sources?

We've got you covered with valuable tips on where to find trustworthy information. Consult reputable academic journals, trusted books, websites, or even engage in conversations with domain experts. And remember, don't simply accept information at face value! Learn to approach it critically, fact-check, and identify any subtle biases.

By embracing the methods and strategies outlined in Chapter 3, you're not merely going through the motions. You're cultivating credibility and making a tangible impact in your field. So, instead of relying on chance, seize the opportunity to elevate your research with the invaluable insights of Chapter 3!

CHAPTER THREE

TIPS & STRATEGIES FOR CONDUCTING EFFECTIVE RESEARCH

UNDERSTANDING THE RESEARCH PROCESS:

THE RESEARCH PROCESS involves several essential steps crucial for conducting effective and reliable research. By following these steps, researchers can make sure their study is well-planned, relevant, and correct. Let's explore each step:

Defining research questions or goals:

The first step in the research process is to clearly define the research questions or goals. This involves identifying the problem or topic of interest that the research aims to address. The research questions should be specific, measurable, achievable, relevant, and time-bound (SMART). This step helps to focus the study and establish its purpose.

Reviewing existing literature:

Before conducting new research, it is important to review existing literature on the chosen topic. This lets researchers identify gaps or areas that require further investigation. By analyzing previous studies and scholarly resources, researchers can also gain a solid understanding of the current state of knowledge in their chosen field.

Developing a research method:

Once the research questions are defined and literature is reviewed, researchers can develop a clear method for their study. This involves deciding on the proper research design, data collection methods (such as surveys, experiments, interviews, or observations), and data analysis techniques. The chosen methods should align with the research goals and ensure the reliability and validity of the findings.

Obtaining ethical approval (if required):

If the research involves human or animal subjects, researchers may need to obtain ethical approval from a proper ethics committee or review board. This step is essential to make sure the research is conducted ethically, and participants are protected from any potential harm.

Collecting and analyzing data:

Once the method is established and ethical approval is obtained, researchers can collect the data needed to address their research questions. This involves gathering information through various methods, such as surveys, experiments, or interviews. After data collection, researchers need to analyze and interpret the data using appropriate statistical or qualitative analysis techniques. This step helps to draw meaningful conclusions from the collected information.

Drawing conclusions and making recommendations:

Based on the analysis of the data, researchers can draw conclusions regarding their research questions or goals. This step involves synthesizing the findings and interpreting them in the existing literature. Researchers should also consider the limitations of their study and identify areas for further research or improvement. Finally, they can make recommendations based on their conclusions, which can be useful for future research or practical applications.

Documenting and distributing findings:

The final step in the research process is documenting and distributing the findings. Researchers should consolidate their research into a comprehensive report or article that includes the research questions, methodology, results, and conclusions. They can then share their work through academic journals, conferences, or other platforms. This step contributes to the wider body of knowledge in the field and allows others to build on the findings.

Conducting effective research involves a systematic and well-structured process. Defining research questions, reviewing literature, developing a clear method, collecting and analyzing data, drawing conclusions, and distributing findings are all vital steps that ensure the reliability and significance of the research. Following this process helps researchers contribute to the advancement of knowledge and meaningfully contribute to their field.

CHOOSING RELIABLE SOURCES:

When writing a book, it is crucial to make sure the information you include is correct and credible. Choosing reliable sources is key to meeting this goal. Here are tips to help you identify trustworthy sources:

Academic Journals: Academic journals are considered highly reliable sources as they undergo rigorous peer review by experts in the field. Look for journals related to the topic of your book and check if the articles are by reputable scholars. You can access academic journals through databases like JSTOR or Google Scholar.

Books: Books written by respected authors and experts in the field are excellent sources of reliable information. Look for books published by renowned publishers or reputable academic institutions. Check credentials and reviews of the authors to evaluate their knowledge and credibility.

Respected Websites: While the internet is a vast source of information, it is important to discern the reliability of websites. Choose websites that are well-established, such as those affiliated with academic institutions, government agencies, or professional organizations. These websites often provide accurate and fact-checked information.

Expert Interviews: Conducting interviews with professionals and subject matter experts adds credibility to your book. Seek interviews with individuals who have recognized knowledge in the topic you are covering. Make sure the interviewees are respected authorities in the field and have a track record of credibility.

Peer-Reviewed Research: Look for studies that have undergone a peer review process. This means that experts in the field have reviewed the research for accuracy and reliability. Peer-reviewed studies can be found in academic journals and databases, providing valuable data and evidence to support your writing.

Cross-Referencing: To determine the validity of a source, cross-reference it with other reliable sources. If multiple reputable sources support the same information, it increases the credibility of that data or idea.

Authoritative Institutions: Seek information from authoritative institutions, such as government agencies, international organizations, or reputable research organizations. These institutions often conduct reliable studies and provide objective data.

Avoiding Biased Sources: Be cautious with sources that present a clear bias or a vested interest in a particular viewpoint. Look for balanced and evidence-based information rather than sources skewed toward a specific agenda.

Citations and References: Evaluate the quality and reliability of sources cited by the author. If the author uses a comprehensive range of reputable sources to support their claims, it increases the reliability of their work.

By using these strategies, you can make sure the information in your book is correct and credible. This will enhance the credibility of your work and provide readers with trustworthy knowledge and insights.

EVALUATING INFORMATION:

Developing Critical Thinking Skills:

In our modern era of information overload, developing critical thinking skills is essential for navigating the vast amount of information available to us. It is crucial to evaluate the relevance, accuracy, and reliability of the information we gather and identify any potential biases in the sources we rely on. This is where fact-checking, cross-referencing, and detecting biases play a significant role. Here are strategies to help you enhance your critical thinking skills in evaluating information:

Relevance:

- **Define your goal:** Clearly identify the purpose of gathering information. This will help you focus on finding relevant sources.

- **Question your sources:** Ask yourself if the information is directly related to your goal. Avoid including irrelevant or tangential information.

Accuracy:

- **Assess the credibility of the source**: Consider the reputation and knowledge of the author, organization, or publication. Look for indicators of quality, such as peer-reviewed journals or reputable news outlets.

- **Fact-check claims and statistics:** Cross-reference the information you find with multiple reliable sources. Check for consistency and make sure the information is supported by evidence.

- **Identify potential biases:** Be aware of any potential agendas or biases that may influence the accuracy of the information. Look for signs of one-sided, subjective, or inflammatory language.

Reliability:

- **Evaluate the timeliness**: Determine if the information is up to date and relevant to the current context. Outdated information may no longer be correct or reliable.

- **Consider the information's origin:** Assess if the source is primary or secondary. Primary sources provide firsthand information, while secondary sources interpret or analyze primary sources.

- **Assess the authority:** Determine if the source has knowledge and credentials on the topic. Analyze if the information follows other reputable sources.

Fact-checking and Cross-referencing:

- **Verify information from multiple sources:** Look for consensus among credible sources. Information consistently reported across various reliable sources is more likely to be correct.

- **Consult experts or specialists:** Reach out to professionals in the field to confirm the information. Their knowledge can provide valuable insights.

- **Utilize fact-checking tools:** Online fact-checking websites and tools can help verify the accuracy of specific claims.

Detecting Biases:

- **Understand the author's perspective:** Research the author's background, affiliations, and potential conflicts of interest. These factors can influence their biases.

- **Analyze the language and tone: Look** for loaded or emotionally charged language that may show a bias. Identify if the author presents a balanced view or presents only one side of the argument.

- **Seek alternative viewpoints:** Expose yourself to varied perspectives from multiple sources to gain a more comprehensive understanding of the topic.

By adopting these strategies for evaluating information, you can develop critical thinking skills that enable you to make informed decisions and form opinions based on reliable and credible sources.

Remember, being critical thinkers helps us become responsible consumers and contributors to the information landscape.

CONDUCTING EFFECTIVE INTERVIEWS:

Interviewing experts in your field can provide you with firsthand insights and valuable information that can greatly enhance your work. Whether you're a journalist, researcher, or simply seeking knowledge, conducting effective interviews is a skill worth mastering. This section will guide you through techniques for preparing interview questions, conducting interviews, and extracting valuable quotes and anecdotes.

Preparing for the Interview:

Research the Expert: Before conducting an interview, it is crucial to thoroughly research the expert and their work. This will help you ask relevant questions and show your knowledge, earning the expert's trust and respect.

Define Your Objectives: Clearly define the goals of your interview. Determine what information you aim to gather, what insights you seek, and what impact the expert's perspective will have on your work. This will guide the formulation of your interview questions.

Create a Structure: Organize your interview questions in a logical structure. Start with broader, introductory questions to establish rapport, and then move toward more specific topics. This structure will ensure a smooth flow during the interview and let you cover all essential points.

Crafting Effective Interview Questions:

Open-Ended Questions: Construct questions that prompt detailed, narrative responses. Open-ended questions encourage experts to elaborate on their thoughts, providing you with rich insights. Avoid questions that can be answered with a simple "yes" or "no."

Probing Questions: Prepare follow-up questions that dive deeper into specific topics. Probing questions help you uncover more details, challenge assumptions, and explore different angles of the interviewee's knowledge.

Personalized Questions: Tailor your questions to the expert's unique experiences and knowledge. Make the interviewee feel valued and acknowledged by asking questions that reflect their specific contributions and perspectives.

Conducting the Interview:

Establish Rapport: Begin the interview by establishing a friendly and comfortable atmosphere. Introduce yourself, express gratitude for their willingness to share their knowledge, and assure them that their insights are highly valued.

Active Listening: Pay close attention to the expert's responses. Active listening involves maintaining eye contact, nodding, and providing verbal cues to show your engagement. This helps build rapport and encourages the expert to open up further.

Follow the Flow: While it's important to follow your prepared questions, don't be afraid to deviate from the script if an interesting line of conversation emerges. Adaptability lets the interview flow naturally and encourages the expert to share additional valuable insights.

Extracting Valuable Quotes and Anecdotes:

Highlight Key Points: During the interview, note down significant quotes, statistics, or anecdotes shared by the expert. These memorable soundbites can add credibility and interest to your final work.

Seek Permission for Quotes: When extracting quotes, ensure you have the interviewee's consent to use their statements. Respect their intellectual property rights and provide them with the opportunity to review the quotes for accuracy.

Contextualize Quotes: Ensure that the quotes you use are properly contextualized within the broader discussion. It is essential to present the expert's statements accurately and in a way that accurately reflects the interviewee's intended message.

Conducting effective interviews with experts in your field can yield valuable insights and information to enhance your work. By researching the expert, crafting thoughtful interview questions, conducting interviews with attention and adaptability, and extracting and contextualizing valuable quotes and anecdotes, you can master the art of interviewing and create compelling content that resonates with your audience.

USING ONLINE RESEARCH TOOLS:

In the digital age, conducting research has become more efficient and correct thanks to the availability of various online tools and resources. This article aims to explore the diverse range of digital tools and resources that can significantly enhance the research process. Using databases, search engines, citation managers, and other technological aids, researchers can maximize their efficiency and ensure the accuracy of their work.

1. Databases:

Databases provide access to a vast collection of scholarly articles, books, reports, and other academic resources. Some popular databases include:

a) PubMed: Specifically designed for biomedical and life sciences research, PubMed offers an extensive collection of articles from scientific journals.

b) JSTOR: JSTOR provides a wide range of academic resources across various disciplines, including humanities, social sciences, and natural sciences.

c) IEEE Xplore: Focusing on technical literature in fields such as engineering, computer science, and information technology, IEEE Xplore is a valuable resource for researchers in these domains.

· · ·

2. Search Engines:

While search engines like Google are widely used, there are specialized search engines specifically tailored for academic research:

a) Google Scholar: Google Scholar is a search engine that specifically indexes scholarly literature, including articles, theses, books, conference papers, and more.

b) Microsoft Academic: Developed by Microsoft, this search engine offers an extensive database of academic publications from various disciplines.

c) BASE (Bielefeld Academic Search Engine): BASE is one of the world's most extensive multidisciplinary search engines, indexing content from institutional repositories, digital libraries, and other academic websites.

3. Citation Managers:

Keeping track of citations and references is crucial when conducting research. Citation managers help researchers organize and format their references efficiently. Popular citation managers include:

a) Zotero: A free, open-source tool that allows researchers to collect, organize, and cite sources in multiple citation styles.

b) Mendeley: Combining reference management with social networking features, Mendeley enables collaboration and discovery of related research.

c) EndNote: A comprehensive reference management software with advanced features such as PDF annotation and integration with other research tools.

4. Technological Aids:

Beyond databases, search engines, and citation managers, researchers can benefit from other digital tools that enhance their research process:

a) Data visualization tools: Tools like Tableau and Infogram help researchers present complex data in a visually appealing and easy-to-understand format.

b) Text analysis tools: Tools like Voyant and Lexos help researchers in analyzing large volumes of text by providing features such as word frequency analysis, topic modeling, and sentiment analysis.

c) Collaboration tools: Tools like Google Docs and Microsoft Teams help with remote collaboration, letting researchers work together in real-time, share documents, and communicate efficiently.

In the digital age, harnessing the power of online research tools is essential to maximize efficiency and accuracy. From databases to search engines, citation managers to technological aids, the range of tools available enables researchers to access a wealth of information, organize their findings, and collaborate effectively. Using these tools, researchers can enhance their research process and produce high-quality work.

ORGANIZING AND ANALYZING RESEARCH:

When conducting research, it is crucial to effectively organize and analyze the vast amount of gathered information. Without proper organization and analysis techniques, research materials can become overwhelming, making it difficult to extract relevant information and draw meaningful conclusions. This section focuses on several effective techniques that can aid researchers in managing their research materials.

Create Research Databases and Libraries: One of the first steps in organizing research materials is creating databases or libraries to store relevant information. These databases can be physical or digital and should be categorized based on the research topic, subtopics, or any other relevant criteria. Within each category, further subcategorize the materials for easy retrieval. This process enables quick access to specific information when needed and prevents loss or misplacement.

Use Reference Management Software: Reference management software such as EndNote, Mendeley, or Zotero can significantly simplify the organization of research materials. These tools let researchers store and organize references, attach relevant documents or notes, and generate properly formatted citations easily. Additionally, they provide features like keyword tagging, full-text search, and collaboration capabilities, enhancing the efficiency and accessibility of research materials.

Use Note-Taking Methods: Taking notes is essential for summarizing important information and highlighting key findings during the research process. Researchers can use various note-taking methods, such as the Cornell method, idea mapping, or outlining, depending on their preferences and requirements. When taking notes, ensure to include relevant reference details and page numbers for easy retrieval later. Additionally, consider using color coding or different fonts to distinguish between different types of information or ideas.

Summarize and Synthesize: As research materials collect, it is essential to summarize and synthesize the information obtained. This involves extracting the key points, arguments, or findings from each source and noting them down in a concise and structured manner. By summarizing and synthesizing, researchers can gain a holistic understanding of the gathered information, identify connections between different sources, and ultimately develop a coherent analysis.

Analyze Data and Draw Conclusions: Once the research materials are organized and summarized, it is crucial to analyze the data and draw conclusions. Data analysis techniques may vary depending on the type of research conducted, such as descriptive statistics, content analysis, or thematic analysis. Through data analysis, researchers can identify patterns, trends, or relationships within the collected information, helping with the formulation of meaningful conclusions and the generation of new knowledge.

Keep Track of Sources: It is essential to maintain a comprehensive list of all the sources consulted during the research process. This includes books, articles, websites, interviews, or any other relevant material. Accurately record the bibliographic details such as author names, publication titles, dates, and page numbers. Keeping track of sources makes sure proper citations can be provided in the research report or academic paper and reduces the chances of accidental plagiarism.

Organizing and analyzing research materials is crucial for effective research. By creating databases, using reference management software, using note-taking methods, summarizing and synthesizing information, analyzing data, and keeping track of sources, researchers can effectively manage and navigate through the overwhelming amount of gathered research materials, leading to more structured and impactful findings.

ETHICAL CONSIDERATIONS IN RESEARCH:

As an author conducting research for your book, it is essential to understand and uphold the ethical responsibilities that come with this process. This chapter aims to provide guidance on various parts of ethical considerations, including proper citation practices, avoiding plagiarism, and respecting the privacy and intellectual property rights of your sources. By adhering to these principles, you can ensure your research is conducted in an ethical and responsible manner.

Proper Citation Practices:

When incorporating ideas, information, or direct quotes from your sources, it is crucial to give credit to the original authors. Proper citation practices not only enforce academic integrity but also show respect for others' work. Follow the proper citation style, such as APA, MLA, or Chicago, ensuring consistency throughout your book. Take care to include complete and correct references, acknowledging the sources that have contributed to your research.

Avoiding Plagiarism:

Plagiarism is a serious offense that undermines the integrity of your work and the original creators. It involves presenting someone else's ideas, words, or works as your own, without proper acknowledgment. To avoid plagiarism, always attribute information and ideas that are rare knowledge to their rightful owners. Use quotation marks for direct quotes and refer to paraphrased content. Additionally, software tools such as plagiarism checkers can help you identify unintentional or accidental occurrences of plagiarism.

Respecting Privacy:

While conducting research, it is crucial to respect the privacy of your sources. Obtain informed consent before using any personal or sensitive information, making sure individuals are aware of how their data will be used. Take reasonable measures to protect the anonymity of your participants, especially when dealing with confidential or sensitive subjects. Respect any requests for confidentiality or anonymity, letting individuals maintain their privacy even after sharing their opinions or experiences.

Respecting Intellectual Property Rights:

Intellectual property rights protect the creations or inventions of individuals or organizations. When using copyrighted material in your research, seek permission from the copyright holders, whether it is for text, images, videos, or other multimedia content. Properly attribute all copyrighted works and avoid using them beyond what is considered fair use. Be mindful of the potential impact on the financial or reputational interests of others when using their intellectual property.

Addressing Ethical Challenges:

During the research process, you may encounter ethical challenges that require careful consideration. For example, balancing the need for accuracy and thoroughness with the potential harm to participants or sources. Consult with research ethics committees, professional organizations, or colleagues with expertise in ethics to navigate complex ethical dilemmas. By seeking guidance, you can ensure your research respects ethical principles and aligns with set standards.

Conducting research for your book comes with a set of ethical responsibilities. Proper citation practices, avoiding plagiarism, respecting privacy, and honoring intellectual property rights are essential parts of ethical considerations in research. By undertaking research in an ethical and responsible manner, you not only maintain your own integrity as an author but also contribute to the overall credibility and advancement of knowledge within your field.

Chapter Summary:

Chapter 3 is all about doing research the right way. It lays out clear steps for you. Start by figuring out your research questions and make sure they're SMART and tied to what you want to learn. Next, look at what others have done to find gaps and learn from their work.

Then, design your research methods, pick how you'll collect data, analyze it, and get ethical approval if you need it. Wrap it all up by making conclusions, giving advice, and sharing what you find.

The chapter also gives you tips on picking good sources. Look at respected academic stuff, talk to experts, use research that others have checked, and watch out for biased sources.

Lastly, it shows you how to look at information with a critical eye. You'll learn how to check facts, spot biases, and make good decisions. By following these tips, you'll make your work better and really add something meaningful to your field.

In our Next Chapter...

In the upcoming Chapter 4, we'll delve into the art of storytelling within the nonfiction genre. Nonfiction need not be composed of monotonous facts or complex ideas. It can be woven with elements that stir emotions and create unforgettable experiences.

In this chapter, we'll guide you in transforming even the most complicated subjects into relatable narratives, making them more accessible and memorable. You'll navigate through our step-by-step process, building a narrative that resonates deeply with readers.

We'll also discuss the importance of this style of writing in today's fast-paced world, shedding light on how to engage readers and keep them invested in your work. We'll examine real-world examples such as

"The Immortal Life of Henrietta Lacks" to see how successful authors have achieved this.

To supplement this, the chapter is packed with useful tips and exercises to enhance your storytelling skills. Despite your experience level, this chapter provides resources to help you craft nonfiction that touches both the heart and the mind. Chapter 4 promises to be a journey into the world of impactful storytelling. So, join us, let's unravel this together!

∽

DEVELOPING A COMPELLING NARRATIVE

THE POWER OF STORYTELLING IN NONFICTION: HOW A COMPELLING NARRATIVE CAN ENHANCE THE IMPACT & EFFECTIVENESS OF NONFICTION WRITING

NONFICTION WRITING IS OFTEN ASSOCIATED with facts, evidence, and logical arguments. However, one should not underestimate the power of storytelling in nonfiction. By incorporating a compelling narrative, nonfiction writers can enhance the impact and effectiveness of their work. This chapter explores how storytelling in nonfiction can engage readers, make complex topics more accessible, evoke emotions, and ultimately leave a lasting impact.

Engaging Readers:

One of the main challenges in nonfiction writing is capturing readers' attention and keeping them engaged throughout the piece. Storytelling in nonfiction lets writers present information in a captivating and relatable manner. By weaving anecdotes, personal experiences, or case studies into their narrative, writers can create a sense of intrigue and curiosity which helps to hook and keep readers.

Making Complex Topics Accessible:

Many nonfiction topics can be complex, technical, or challenging to grasp for readers who lack prior knowledge in the subject. However, storytelling can serve as a bridge between unfamiliar ideas and readers. By using storytelling techniques, writers can simplify complex ideas, break them down into digestible pieces, and present them in a more understandable and relatable way. Through narratives, writers can build connections, draw analogies, or use metaphors that resonate with readers, letting them connect the dots and comprehend abstract or intricate ideas.

Eliciting Emotions:

While nonfiction is primarily concerned with facts and information, emotion plays a crucial role in human perception and understanding. Storytelling, in nonfiction, is a powerful tool for evoking emotion. By incorporating personal stories or interviews with real people, writers can add depth, empathy, and a human touch to their work. Emotionally resonant stories can trigger empathy, compassion, or even anger or frustration, prompting readers to feel a personal connection to the subject and motivating them to act or change their perspectives.

Leaving a Lasting Impact:

The ultimate goal of nonfiction writing is to inform and persuade readers. By employing storytelling techniques, writers can go beyond mere information transfer and leave a lasting impact on readers. An engaging narrative can embed key messages, lessons, or insights within the reader's memory. It enables readers to remember, reflect, and apply the information long after they finish reading. People often remember stories better than a list of facts or statistics, making storytelling a more powerful tool for creating lasting impressions.

Storytelling in nonfiction is a potent tool that can enhance the impact and effectiveness of the writing. The ability to engage readers, make complex topics accessible, evoke emotions, and leave a lasting impact makes storytelling an indispensable element of nonfiction writing. By incorporating narratives, writers can create a connection between the facts and the reader, making them active participants in the story being told. So the power of storytelling in nonfiction cannot be overlooked, as it has the potential to transform readers' understanding, perspectives, and actions.

UNDERSTANDING THE READER'S ENGAGEMENT: THE POWER OF NARRATIVE STRUCTURE IN CAPTURING ATTENTION

In today's fast-paced world with plenty of information at our fingertips, capturing readers' attention has become an increasingly challenging task. However, one timeless and effective technique for engaging readers is through a well-crafted narrative structure. This chapter will explore the importance of capturing readers' attention through storytelling and its potential to increase interest and understanding.

Engaging the Reader:

Capturing readers' attention is the first crucial step in making sure they remain interested and engaged throughout the narrative. By using a well-crafted narrative structure, writers can effectively hook readers from the start. This can be done through an intriguing opening, a compelling conflict or question, or even an unexpected twist. When readers are captivated by an engaging beginning, they are more likely to continue reading and invest their focus and emotions into the story.

Emotional Connection:

A well-crafted narrative structure lets writers establish deep emotional connections with readers. Through the use of relatable characters, vivid descriptions, and evocative language, writers can immerse readers in the story's world, making them feel invested in the outcomes and experiences of the characters. This emotional connection not only fosters a sense of empathy but also enhances understanding and retention of the story's message or themes.

Enhanced Understanding:

A cohesive and well-structured narrative can significantly enhance readers' understanding of complex ideas or ideas. By presenting information in a narrative form, writers can break down complex ideas into relatable and understandable terms. Using characters, plot, and storytelling techniques can help readers grasp even the most abstract or intricate ideas. Narratives provide a context that aids in connecting ideas, letting readers see the bigger picture and comprehend the relevance of the information being presented.

Sustained Interest:

A well-crafted narrative structure has the potential to sustain readers' interest throughout the entire piece. By integrating suspense, tension, and pacing, writers can keep readers eagerly turning the pages, craving to know what happens next. This sustained interest makes sure readers remain engaged and invested until the very end, increasing the likelihood of them absorbing and internalizing the story's message or purpose.

By analyzing the importance of capturing readers' attention through a well-crafted narrative structure, it becomes clear how storytelling can significantly enhance interest and understanding. Whether it be through an intriguing opening, establishing emotional connections, fostering comprehension, or sustaining interest, narratives have the power to captivate readers and make the reading experience both enriching and memorable. Writers should strive to harness the potential of narrative structure to effectively engage their audience and create impactful content.

CRAFTING A CAPTIVATING NARRATIVE STRUCTURE: STEP-BY-STEP GUIDANCE ON DEVELOPING A STRONG NARRATIVE FRAMEWORK

Step 1: Determine your Purpose and Message

Before diving into crafting a narrative structure, it's crucial to identify your purpose and message. Ask yourself what you want to convey to your readers and what emotions or ideas you want to evoke. Clarifying your purpose will help you create a strong foundation for your narrative.

Step 2: Choose a Narrative Arc

A narrative arc provides a structure for your story, taking readers on a journey from beginning to end. Common narrative arcs include the classic three-act structure (introduction, rising action, climax, falling action, and resolution) or the hero's journey (a protagonist embarks on a transformative quest).

Step 3: Define the Key Elements: Characters, Setting, and Conflict

Develop compelling characters that readers can relate to, care about, and root for. Give them distinct personalities, motivations, and flaws. Create a vivid and immersive setting that complements the story and adds depth to your narrative. Introduce conflict that drives the plot forward and keeps readers engaged.

Step 4: Establish a Hook

Grab your readers' attention from the beginning by starting with a hook—a captivating opening sentence or paragraph that piques their curiosity or introduces a conflict or mystery. A strong hook will make readers want to continue reading.

Step 5: Build Rising Action

The rising action forms the bulk of your narrative and should gradually escalate the conflict while introducing new obstacles and challenges for your characters. Use tension, suspense, and pacing effectively to keep readers engaged. Each scene should propel the story forward and reveal new information or develop the characters.

Step 6: Create Climax and Resolution

The climax is the turning point of your story, where the conflict reaches its peak. Choose a significant event or revelation that will leave a lasting impact on readers. Following the climax, provide a resolution that wraps up loose ends and offers closure to the story. Make sure the resolution remains consistent with the narrative's purpose and message.

Step 7: Consider Narrative Techniques

Incorporate narrative techniques such as foreshadowing, flashbacks, or multiple perspectives to add complexity and depth to your story. However, use them sparingly and purposefully to avoid over-whelming your readers.

Step 8: Edit and Revise

Once you have crafted the narrative structure, revise and edit your work. Pay attention to clarity, coherence, pacing, and consistency. Make sure each element and scene contributes to the overall narrative and supports the purpose and message you defined earlier.

Step 9: Seek Feedback

Share your narrative with trusted friends, colleagues, or writing groups to gather feedback. Listen to their suggestions and criticism while remembering your artistic vision. Constructive feedback can help you strengthen your narrative structure and make it more captivating.

Step 10: Refine and Polish

Using the feedback received, refine your narrative structure further. Polish your prose, dialogue, and descriptions to make them engaging and vivid. Check for any plot holes or inconsistencies and address them. Take the time to perfect your narrative structure to create a captivating and coherent story that enthralls readers from beginning to end.

USING STORYTELLING TECHNIQUES:

Once upon a time, in the small town of Oakville, lived a young boy named Max. Max was a curious and imaginative child, always yearning for adventure. He had a deep admiration for his grandfather, who was an incredible storyteller.

Every Sunday afternoon, Max would eagerly rush to his grandfather's house, ready to listen to another captivating tale. His grandfather had a unique way of bringing characters to life, making them feel like old friends. Each story was filled with intricate details about their personalities, their hopes, and their dreams.

One fateful Sunday, Max's grandfather began telling a story unlike any other. It was a tale about a young girl named Lily, who lived in a mystical forest known as Whispering Woods. Lily was vibrant and full of zest, always seeking excitement.

As the story progressed, Max noticed how his grandfather cleverly weaved in plot twists and turns, making it impossible to predict what would happen next. He felt his heart race with anticipation as Lily stumbled upon a hidden treasure at the heart of the forest.

With every word, Max's grandfather skillfully built tension, keeping him on the edge of his seat. Max was so engrossed in the story that he could almost hear the rustling leaves and feel the mystical aura of Whispering Woods. He longed to join Lily on her adventure, to experience the magic for himself.

In the midst of all the excitement, Max realized that his grandfather was not just telling a story, but also imparting valuable lessons. He understood that character development was vital in evoking empathy and creating emotional connections. Through the ups and downs of Lily's journey, Max learned about perseverance, friendship, and the importance of embracing one's true self.

As Max grew older, he honed his storytelling skills, like his grandfather. He knew that by mastering character development, plot progression, and building tension, he could effectively convey information and evoke emotional connections. Through storytelling, Max discovered the power of narrating intricate tales that could touch people's hearts, like his grandfather's stories had touched his.

And so, like his grandfather had inspired him, Max inspired others. He shared his stories of adventure, lessons, and dreams, touching the lives of countless others. Max realized that by using storytelling techniques, he could create a profound impact on individuals and communities, fostering understanding, empathy, and compassion.

From that day forward, Max understood that by embracing the art of storytelling, he could leave a lasting legacy, connecting hearts and minds, and bringing joy to the world.

BALANCING FACTS & STORYTELLING:

In the realm of communication, storytelling has long been recognized as a powerful tool to engage and captivate audiences. However, a delicate balance needs to be struck when incorporating storytelling elements into narratives that aim to convey factual information. This challenge, of maintaining factual accuracy while infusing the narrative with storytelling elements, requires careful consideration to make sure the audience is both entertained and well-informed. In this section, we will examine this balance, exploring the significance of factual accuracy and how storytelling techniques can enhance the delivery of information.

Factual Accuracy:

Factual accuracy is the foundation on which any narrative rests. It involves presenting information that is proven, supported by evidence, and free from bias. In an era of misinformation and fake news, maintaining factual accuracy in storytelling becomes increasingly vital. Facts are fundamental to building trust with audiences and establishing credibility as a storyteller. Without this foundation, any narrative risks losing its effectiveness and impact.

Storytelling Elements:

Storytelling, on the other hand, introduces a human element into information delivery, making it more relatable, memorable, and engaging. By using techniques such as character development, conflict, and suspense, storytellers can create a rich and immersive experience for audiences. These elements heighten emotional connection, letting the information resonate on a deeper level and increasing the likelihood of long-term retention. Storytelling enhances the accessibility and appeal of factual narratives.

The Challenge:

Balancing storytelling elements with factual accuracy poses a unique challenge. The storyteller must consider the extent and manner in which fiction is woven into the narrative. While creative liberties can make the story more compelling, they should not compromise the integrity of the facts being presented. Thus, the storyteller must carefully select the storytelling techniques that work in harmony with the factual information.

Strategies for Balancing:

To balance factual accuracy and storytelling elements, several strategies can be employed. Foremost, thorough research is essential. Fact-checking and verifying sources is crucial to make sure the information presented is true and reliable. Additionally, storytelling techniques should be used judiciously and appropriately, without overshadowing the facts. A clear distinction should be made between the factual information and any fictional elements introduced. Transparency is vital in maintaining credibility and avoiding confusion.

Narratives should aim at presenting diverse perspectives and acknowledging potential biases. Storytelling that acknowledges these nuances adds depth and authenticity to the narrative, and fosters a sense of trust among the audience.

Achieving a balance between storytelling and factual accuracy is a complex yet critical task. The art of combining information and emotion in narratives can create impactful and compelling stories that resonate with audiences. By maintaining factual accuracy and using appropriate storytelling elements, storytellers can effectively connect with their audience, leaving a lasting impression while also conveying valuable information. It is through the mastery of this delicate balance that the true potential of storytelling can be realized.

CASE STUDIES & EXAMPLES ILLUSTRATING THE IMPACT OF STORYTELLING IN NONFICTION

Case Study 1: "The Immortal Life of Henrietta Lacks" by Rebecca Skloot

One powerful example of storytelling in nonfiction is "The Immortal Life of Henrietta Lacks" by Rebecca Skloot. This book tells the true story of Henrietta Lacks, an African-American woman whose cells were harvested without her consent in the 1950s and used for groundbreaking medical research. Skloot skillfully weaves together Henrietta's personal story, the scientific breakthroughs enabled by her cells, and the ethical questions raised by the case.

By employing storytelling techniques, Skloot brings Henrietta and her family to life, humanizing their experiences and struggles. This narrative approach lets readers emotionally connect with the characters and understand the larger implications of scientific research. Skloot's storytelling effectively communicates the complex ethical issues surrounding medical consent and explores the racial disparities in healthcare.

Case Study 2: "Into Thin Air" by Jon Krakauer

Another compelling case study is Jon Krakauer's "Into Thin Air." This nonfiction book recounts the devastating 1996 Mount Everest disaster, in which multiple climbers lost their lives. Krakauer, an experienced mountaineer who was part of the ill-fated expedition, tells the story from a first-person perspective, using vivid description and personal anecdotes to transport readers to the treacherous slopes of Everest.

Krakauer's storytelling enhances the understanding of the physical and mental challenges faced by mountaineers and the dangers inherent in attempting such a feat. By incorporating captivating narratives, he effectively communicates the risks, the thrills, and the human elements of climbing Everest. This approach lets readers grasp the intricacies of high-altitude mountaineering and the moral dilemmas that arise in extreme situations.

Case Study 3: TED Talks by Chimamanda Ngozi Adichie

Chimamanda Ngozi Adichie, a renowned Nigerian author and speaker, has delivered inspiring TED Talks that exemplify the impact of storytelling in nonfiction. In her talk "The Danger of a Single Story," she shares personal anecdotes about growing up in Nigeria and the danger of relying on stereotypes and limited perspectives. Adichie's storytelling approach engages the audience, letting them connect emotionally with her experiences, and highlights the importance of diverse narratives to foster understanding and eradicate prejudices.

Through her narratives, Adichie effectively communicates complex ideas about the power of storytelling and challenges the audience to question their own assumptions. Her talk serves as an illustrative example of how well-crafted narratives can dismantle preconceived notions and promote empathy and inclusivity in society.

These case studies and examples show the impactful role of storytelling in nonfiction. By using narrative techniques, authors like Rebecca Skloot, Jon Krakauer, and Chimamanda Ngozi Adichie effectively communicate complex ideas and information, creating engaging, relatable, and memorable experiences for readers and listeners.

Practical Exercises & Tips:

Develop a strong premise: A solid nonfiction story starts with a captivating premise. Practice brainstorming various ideas and selecting the one that resonates with you the most. Write a one-sentence summary of your premise to keep it focused and concise.

Create compelling characters: Even in nonfiction, characters play a crucial role in engaging readers. Practice observing people around you, or interview individuals related to your story. Note their distinct personalities, quirks, and motivations. Incorporate these elements into your writing to make your characters relatable and memorable.

Use descriptive language: Enhance your storytelling by using vivid and sensory language. Practice describing scenes, settings, and emotions using metaphorical language, rich imagery, and powerful adjectives. This will help bring your story to life and engage readers on a deeper level.

Incorporate dialogue: Dialogue breathes life into a nonfiction story, making it more engaging and authentic. Practice capturing conversations by listening to people around you or recording interviews. Pay attention to speech patterns, mannerisms, and the unique voices of your subjects. Use dialogue tags and formatting to create natural and dynamic conversations.

Employ storytelling techniques: Nonfiction writing can benefit from various storytelling techniques like foreshadowing, suspense, and flashbacks. Practice incorporating these elements into your work to add depth and intrigue. Experiment with different narrative structures, such as starting in medias res or using a chronological approach, to enhance the flow and impact of your writing.

Establish a clear structure: Structure is essential in nonfiction storytelling to guide readers through your narrative. Practice outlining your story before writing, identifying key points and their order. Consider using subheadings or sections to break up your text and add clarity. Ensure a logical flow, making it easy for readers to follow and understand your story.

Edit and revise: Effective storytelling is often the result of meticulous editing and revision. Practice the art of self-editing by critically reviewing your work for clarity, coherence, and conciseness. Remove unnecessary details, trim redundant sentences, and refine your language to create a more polished and impactful piece of writing.

Read widely: Improve your storytelling skills by immersing yourself in a variety of nonfiction literature. Read books, articles, and essays from different genres and styles. Observe how accomplished authors structure their stories, create compelling characters, and use descriptive language. Take inspiration from their techniques and adapt them to your own writing.

Seek feedback: Feedback from others can be invaluable in honing your storytelling skills. Practice sharing your work with trusted friends, writing groups, or online communities. Ask for specific feedback on areas you want to improve, such as character development, pacing, or clarity. Incorporate their suggestions into your revisions to enhance your storytelling.

Practice, practice, practice: Like any skill, storytelling improves with practice. Set aside regular time for writing and storytelling exercises. Challenge yourself to write short stories, personal essays, or creative anecdotes to sharpen your nonfiction storytelling skills. Embrace failures as learning opportunities and keep pushing yourself to become a better storyteller.

Chapter Summary:

Chapter 4 took you on a journey into the heart of storytelling in nonfiction. You might have thought that nonfiction was just a heap of dry facts, but we broke that myth wide open. It was all about putting life into those facts and making them sing. You learned how to get readers not just interested but hooked.

First, we talked about how stories could catch readers and keep them coming back for more. We looked at real-life examples and interviews to show you how even the most technical stuff could feel real and close to home. We taught you how to make people feel something, and that's how you left a lasting mark.

But how did you build a great story? We didn't leave you sweating; we gave you a step-by-step guide. From figuring out what you wanted to say to building the story from the ground up, we showed you how to do it all.

We also talked about why it was so important to get your story right those days. It was a noisy world, and you had to make people pay attention. We showed you how to pull them in and keep them with you.

We even took a trip to Oakville, where young Max learned how to tell stories from his grandfather. You saw how storytelling can change lives and connect people.

We dug into the nitty-gritty of balancing facts and storytelling. You had to be careful not to let the story take over the facts, but we showed you how to get it just right.

And we looked at real-world examples like "The Immortal Life of Henrietta Lacks" to show you how storytelling could make even complex ideas come alive.

Last but not least, we gave you hands-on tips and exercises to help you sharpen your storytelling skills. We covered everything from character creation to editing, reading widely, and continuous practice.

Chapter 4 gave you everything you needed to take your nonfiction to the next level. If you wanted to move people with your writing, we had the tools to help you do it. We learned the magic of storytelling together!

In our Next Chapter...

If you seek to craft a book that captivates readers from the first word, then Chapter 5 is your starting point.

Aptly titled "Creating A Strong Outline: Organizing Your Book's Content in A Logical & Engaging Manner to Keep Readers Invested," this pivotal chapter lays the foundation, much like the cornerstone of a house.

Think you can simply dive into writing and improvise along the way? Think again! This chapter reveals why such an approach is like constructing a house without laying the groundwork. A robust outline is indispensable to keep everything intact.

Consider it as your roadmap for the entire adventure, ensuring a seamless writing journey without abrupt leaps or dead ends. Naturally, you want your readers to relish the experience, right? Well, an outline empowers you to craft a story not only thrilling but also coherent. But wait, there's more!

An outline fuels excitement by unveiling unexpected twists, leaving readers perpetually intrigued. It serves as a medium to acquaint yourself with your characters – their identities, desires, and reasons for readers to care about them. What about those profound ideas you yearn to share?

Whether it's love, life, politics, or any other subject, meticulous planning is imperative. An outline equips you with precisely that ability. And let's not forget about the flow! Your story must effortlessly glide along, ensuring readers remain engrossed.

This chapter will guide you in mastering that art as well.

So, if you aspire to create something remarkable, Chapter 5 is where you begin. It unlocks the key to everything – captivating readers, forging connections with characters, and conveying your profound ideas. Don't miss out on this transformative opportunity; it's where the magic begins!

∼

CREATING A STRONG OUTLINE: ORGANIZING YOUR BOOK'S CONTENT IN A LOGICAL & ENGAGING MANNER TO KEEP READERS INVESTED

THE IMPORTANCE OF A STRONG OUTLINE: KEEPING READERS ENGAGED & INVESTED IN YOUR BOOK FROM THE BEGINNING TO THE END.

WHEN EMBARKING on the journey of writing a book, many aspiring authors may be tempted to dive headfirst into their creative process without spending ample time on outlining. However, what they fail to recognize is that a strong outline serves as the backbone of any compelling narrative, making sure readers remain engaged and invested from the beginning to the end of their literary voyage. In this article, we will explore the significance of a well-structured outline and its impact on the reader's experience.

First, a well-crafted outline provides a roadmap for the writer, guiding them through the twists and turns of their narrative. It makes sure the story flows smoothly, with no abrupt jumps or inconsistencies. By outlining the major plot points, character development arcs, and thematic progression, authors can maintain a coherent storyline that captivates readers. This structured approach lets writers establish a logical flow of events, preventing them from straying off track and losing the readers' interest.

An outline is instrumental in maintaining a constant sense of tension and anticipation throughout the book. By strategically placing compelling plot twists, character revelations, and climactic moments, the outline enables authors to create peaks and valleys in the narrative, stimulating curiosity and emotional investment. These well-placed elements keep readers on their toes, eager to uncover the next unexpected turn. Without an outline, the story may meander aimlessly, losing its impact and leaving readers feeling disconnected and disinterested.

In addition to maintaining the reader's engagement, a strong outline lets authors carefully develop their characters. By predefining each character's traits, motivations, and growth arcs, writers can establish believable and relatable personalities. Fleshed-out characters with distinct voices and compelling backstories add depth and dimension to the story, enabling readers to form emotional connections. A lack of character development, which often results from a weak or non-existent outline, can leave readers feeling apathetic toward the characters, hindering their investment in the overall story.

An outline makes sure important themes and messages are effectively conveyed to readers. By outlining the symbolic elements, underlying metaphors, and thematic progression, authors can craft a thought-provoking narrative that resonates with the audience. Whether exploring themes of love, loss, or political turmoil, a well-structured outline enables consistent exploration and integration of these ideas. Without a solid roadmap, the book risks becoming a mere collection of loosely connected scenes, failing to engage readers on a deeper intellectual or emotional level.

A strong outline is the foundation on which a compelling book is built. It guides the writer, ensuring a cohesive and well-paced storyline. It immerses readers in a world of tension and anticipation, leaving them eager to continue their literary journey. A carefully outlined narrative also helps with the development of relatable characters and effective exploration of themes, enhancing the reader's investment in the story. So, authors must recognize the importance of dedicating time and effort to crafting a strong outline, as it serves as the key to keeping readers engaged and invested in their book from beginning to end.

THE SIGNIFICANCE OF SELECTING A LOGICAL FLOW FOR A BOOK

Books, as a medium of communication and storytelling, have the power to captivate the minds and intrigue the hearts of readers. To effectively convey thoughts, ideas, and narratives, authors must carefully consider the logical flow of their writing. The choice of a logical flow plays a crucial role in maintaining readers' interest, ensuring comprehension, and enhancing the overall impact of the book. In this chapter, we will explore the importance of selecting a logical flow for a book and the benefits it brings to both the author and the reader.

Enhancing Reader Engagement:

- A logical flow in a book helps readers connect with the content.
- Following a cohesive structure enables readers to follow the storyline or argument smoothly.
- Proper sequencing of events or ideas generates anticipation and keeps readers engaged.

Promoting Comprehension:

- A logical flow helps readers understand the author's intended message.
- Clear organization aids readers in grasping complex ideas, themes, or fictional narratives.
- An organized structure prevents confusion and ensures a seamless reading experience.

Ensuring Coherence:

- A logical flow lets ideas be presented systematically and coherently.

- It enables the author to support arguments, provide evidence, and build a strong case.
- Coherence makes sure readers can easily follow the author's thought process and draw connections between different ideas.

Maximizing Impact:

- A logical flow amplifies the impact of a book.
- Proper pacing builds tension, creates climactic moments, and delivers emotional impact effectively.
- An organized narrative structure can evoke empathy, provoke thought, or inspire action, leaving a lasting impression on readers.

The significance of selecting a logical flow cannot be overstated when writing a book. A well-structured and logically sequenced book not only enhances reader engagement but also promotes comprehension and coherence throughout the narrative. It maximizes the overall impact of the book by delivering impactful moments and leaving a lasting impression on readers. As authors, it is essential to carefully consider the choice of a logical flow to make sure our writing resonates with our audience and fulfills its purpose.

SEVERAL METHODS CAN BE EMPLOYED TO DETERMINE THE MOST EFFECTIVE ORGANIZATION

Chronological Order:

Organizing a book based on the passage of time is a common way to structure a narrative. This approach entails presenting events and information in the order they occurred, creating a clear timeline for readers to follow. By using chronological order, authors can establish a sense of progression that helps readers understand the development and unfolding of the story.

One advantage of using chronological order is that it provides a clear timeline for readers to follow. By presenting events in the order they occurred, readers can easily grasp the sequence of events and understand how one event leads to another. This clarity helps avoid confusion and enables readers to immerse themselves in the story without constant page flipping or backtracking.

Another advantage of using chronological order is that it establishes a sense of progression. The passage of time becomes a thread that ties the story together, letting readers witness the growth and evolution of characters, places, or ideas. This sense of progression can create anticipation and engagement, as readers eagerly follow the developments of the narrative.

Genres that benefit greatly from chronological order include biographies, historical accounts, and travelogues. In a biography, readers can trace the subject's life journey from birth to significant achievements or milestones. The chronological order lets readers understand how various experiences shaped the subject, providing a comprehensive understanding of their life.

Historical accounts also benefit from chronological order as they showcase the progression of events and convey a sense of how historical developments unfolded over time. By arranging events chronologically, authors can effectively analyze the causes and effects of historical events, leading to a deeper understanding of the topic.

Travelogues, which recount a traveler's journey, often follow chronological order as it lets readers follow the traveler's experiences from one location to another. This structure lets readers feel like they are experiencing the journey themselves, as they move along with the narrator from place to place, capturing the essence of the travel experience.

However, there are potential drawbacks to using chronological order. Maintaining reader engagement can be challenging, particularly when the events being described are not inherently exciting or gripping. Authors must use creative techniques to keep readers interested, such as foreshadowing future events or using descriptive language to evoke emotions or intrigue.

Not all topics lend themselves well to a chronological structure. Abstract or philosophical subjects, for example, may not have a linear timeline that can be easily presented in a chronological order. In such cases, authors may need to explore alternative structures, such as thematic or episodic arrangements, to effectively convey the information.

Organizing a book based on the passage of time through chronological order offers several advantages. It provides a clear timeline for readers to follow, establishes a sense of progression, and works well in genres such as biographies, historical accounts, and travelogues. However, maintaining reader engagement and the limited application in certain topics can pose challenges that authors need to overcome.

Problem-Solution Format:

In a problem-solution format, the author first presents a problem or challenge faced by the readers, and then offers corresponding solutions or strategies to overcome it. This format is highly effective in engaging readers as it captures their attention by addressing the specific challenges they may encounter.

The benefits of using the problem-solution format are numerous. First, it immediately grabs the reader's attention by acknowledging their concerns and providing a sense of relevance. By presenting challenges, it helps readers to identify with the problem and creates a sense of empathy. Providing actionable advice and solutions offers readers practical ways to tackle the problem, making the content more meaningful and likely to be started.

Various genres can effectively use the problem-solution format. Self-help books, for example, often address common challenges such as stress management, relationship issues, or career advice. Instructional guides, whether for learning a new skill or improving existing ones, often use a problem-solution framework. Additionally, business books often present challenges faced by organizations, offering solutions to improve performance or overcome specific obstacles.

However, there are potential challenges in implementing the problem-solution format. First, the author must address a wide range of problems to cater to a diverse audience. This requires thorough research and a comprehensive understanding of the target readership. Additionally, the author needs to avoid repetitiveness in presenting solutions. It is crucial to provide a range of strategies and not rely on a single approach for solving every problem. Last, ensuring cohesive solutions can be a challenge, particularly when dealing with complex or multifaceted issues. The author must carefully analyze the problem and solve that address all underlying parts.

Thematic Progression:

Thematic progression refers to the practice of organizing a book or literary work based on common themes or subject areas. This technique lets authors connect ideas, develop a coherent narrative, and offer readers a deeper understanding of their chosen topics. By structuring a book thematically, authors can provide a sense of continuity and coherence that helps readers follow the flow of ideas.

One of the main benefits of thematic progression is the ability to interconnect ideas throughout a book. By structuring a work around common themes, authors can explore different parts of a topic, gradually building on earlier ideas and creating a more comprehensive understanding. This interconnectedness strengthens the overall message or argument being presented.

For example, in an essay collection focused on environmental issues, each essay may explore a different part of the topic. One essay might delve into the consequences of deforestation, while another might investigate the impact of plastic waste on marine life. By organizing these essays thematically, the author creates a cohesive narrative that lets readers follow the progression of ideas and understand the interconnectedness of environmental challenges.

Thematic progression is commonly used in various genres, including essay collections, anthology-based works, and novels with multiple storylines. In essay collections, authors often write group essays based on related themes, such as politics, culture, or personal experiences.

This helps readers navigate the diverse range of topics and allows for a more nuanced exploration of each theme.

Anthology-based works, whether they are collections of short stories, poems, or essays, often use thematic progression to create a unified reading experience. By organizing pieces around common subjects or motifs, editors can establish a coherent thread throughout the anthology, enhancing the overall impact.

Novels with multiple storylines can also benefit from thematic progression. Authors may choose to structure their book around interconnected themes, as well as interweaving plotlines. This technique allows for the exploration of various perspectives and themes, providing a rich and multi-dimensional reading experience.

While thematic progression can be an effective tool for organizing a book, there are potential limitations to consider. One limitation is the need for diversity within themes. If a book becomes too focused on a single theme or subject area, it can be monotonous for readers. To overcome this, authors must carefully select and develop a range of themes that captivate a broad readership.

Additionally, successfully starting thematic progression requires thoughtful planning for transitions between themes. Smooth and cohesive transitions are crucial to maintaining reader engagement and preventing disorientation. Authors must consider the flow of ideas and make sure each theme is introduced and concluded in a satisfactory way.

Finally, sustaining reader interest throughout a book organized thematically can be challenging. Authors must balance offering fresh perspectives on a theme while avoiding repetition. Introducing new ideas, perspectives, or subtopics within each theme can help maintain reader engagement and prevent the work from feeling stagnant.

Thematic progression lets authors organize their books based on common themes or subject areas, leading to the development of interconnected ideas and a coherent narrative. This technique is commonly used in genres such as essay collections, anthology-based works, and novels with multiple storylines. However, authors should consider the need for diversity within themes, carefully plan transitions, and work to maintain reader interest throughout the book. By doing so, authors can create a compelling and engaging reading experience for their audience.

Hybrid Approaches:

In the realm of organizing information in books or other texts, a hybrid approach involves using a combination of methods to enhance overall effectiveness and readability. By blending different structural formats, authors can create a cohesive and engaging narrative that captures the reader's attention. This approach allows for a more dynamic exploration of the content and can effectively cater to various audiences.

One scenario where hybrid approaches can be effective is when authors use a combination of chronological order and thematic sections. This method is useful when presenting historical events. By organizing the chapters chronologically, readers can follow the timeline of events, while thematic sections help to highlight specific parts, themes, or individuals related to those events. This approach provides a comprehensive perspective and helps readers in understanding the broader context.

Another effective hybrid approach is the problem-solution format within a broader thematic framework. This method is commonly used in self-help or instructional books. Authors introduce a topic or theme, discuss the problems associated with it, present possible solutions, and then repeat the theme within a broader framework. This approach helps readers contextualize the solutions and apply them in various situations.

Successful authors who employed hybrid approaches in their works include Malcolm Gladwell and Yuval Noah Harari. Gladwell's book "Outliers" combines storytelling with research and statistical analysis to explain the factors that contribute to extraordinary success. Similarly, Harari's "Sapiens" uses a blend of historical narrative, scientific speculation, and philosophical inquiry to explore the evolution of humankind. By adopting a hybrid approach, these authors captivated readers with a combination of storytelling, factual information, and thematic exploration.

Experimentation and finding the most suitable combination of methods for a book's content and goals are crucial. Authors should consider the target audience, specific subject matter, and desired impact when deciding on the hybrid approach. It is important to strike a balance between different methods, making sure no format overwhelms the others. By striking this balance, authors can create a unique and engaging reading experience that effectively conveys their message.

Hybrid approaches in organizing information offer exciting possibilities for authors. By combining different methods such as chronological order with thematic sections or using a problem-solution format within a broader thematic framework, authors can enhance the organization of their work. Examples from successful authors illustrate the potential of this approach. Emphasizing experimentation and seeking the most suitable combination for the book's content and goals is essential. In embracing hybrid approaches, authors can create compelling narratives that resonate with readers and leave a lasting impact.

Selecting a logical flow for a book is of paramount importance in ensuring a seamless reading experience for the audience. Throughout this discussion, we have explored three effective methods for organizing content: chronological order, problem-solution format, and thematic progression.

Chronological order presents information in a step-by-step way, enabling readers to follow the sequence of events or ideas easily. This method works well for narratives, historical accounts, and biographies, as it lets the audience grasp the progression of the story or analysis.

The problem-solution format is ideal for books that aim to address specific issues or challenges. By presenting a problem and then providing a solution, authors can engage readers in a practical and interactive manner. This method encourages active thinking and problem-solving, making it particularly effective for self-help books, instructional guides, and persuasive texts.

Thematic progression, on the other hand, organizes content based on common themes or ideas. This method lets authors explore various parts of a topic and provide a holistic understanding to readers. It is especially suitable for scholarly works, philosophical treatises, and books that delve into complex ideas.

Authors must carefully consider their content, goals, and target audience to determine the most effective organization for their book. By taking the time to analyze these factors, authors can make sure their chosen method aligns with their intentions and resonates with their readers.

A well-structured book not only enhances the reader's experience but also improves comprehension and overall impact. When content flows logically and coherently, readers can effortlessly navigate through the material, keeping information more effectively. A well-organized book can leave a lasting impression on readers, influencing their thoughts, emotions, and actions long after they have read.

The choice of a logical flow for a book is a critical decision that authors must make. By considering the three methods discussed - chronological order, problem-solution format, and thematic progression - authors can determine the most suitable organizational approach for their content. Ultimately, a well-structured book can significantly enhance the reader's experience, comprehension, and overall impact, making it an essential part of the writing process.

INTRODUCING KEY CONCEPTS & THEMES:

In any piece of writing, the early introduction of key concepts and themes is paramount. This is especially true for books as it sets the stage for the rest of the narrative and enables readers to fully comprehend and engage with the core ideas effortlessly. By incorporating these fundamental elements from the outset, authors can establish a strong foundation on which the entire book can be built.

The significance of introducing main ideas and themes early on lies in it establishing a clear roadmap for readers to navigate through the book. By presenting key ideas within the initial pages or chapters, authors provide readers with a framework to understand the subsequent content. This not only helps readers to grasp and contextualize the overall storyline but also enhances their reading experience by providing them with a sense of direction.

Additionally, early introduction of ideas and themes enables readers to form connections between the core ideas and the narrative elements that follow. When readers are exposed to the main ideas right from the beginning, their understanding of the subsequent events becomes deeper and more nuanced. This allows for a more holistic interpretation of the overall message the author aims to convey.

Introducing key concepts and themes early on lays the groundwork for further exploration and development of these ideas throughout the book. By establishing the importance of these topics from the start, authors create a sense of "promise" to the readers, assuring them that the book will delve into these core ideas extensively. This promise increases reader engagement and anticipation, keeping them invested in the narrative.

By introducing main ideas and themes early, authors can build tension and suspense. By immediately drawing readers into the core ideas, authors create a sense of curiosity and intrigue, urging readers to continue reading to fully comprehend the intricacies of these ideas. This enhances the overall reading experience and encourages readers to remain engaged and invested throughout the whole book.

The significance of introducing key concepts and themes early in a book cannot be overstated. By doing so, authors provide readers with a clear roadmap, enable deeper understanding of later events, lay the groundwork for further exploration, and increase reader engagement. Through this deliberate and strategic introduction of core ideas, authors establish a strong foundation for their work, setting the stage for a rich and captivating reading experience.

STRATEGIES FOR BALANCING CHAPTERS & SECTIONS:

When structuring a book, it's important to create a seamless and balanced reading experience for your audience. One way to achieve this is by carefully dividing your book into chapters and sections. This process involves maintaining a smooth flow of information and preventing readers from feeling overwhelmed or disengaged. Here are strategies to help you achieve this balance:

Consider the length: Determine a proper length for each chapter and section. Long chapters can be intimidating to readers and may cause them to lose interest. But short chapters might disrupt the flow of the narrative. Aim for a consistent length that lets readers digest the content comfortably.

Organize by theme or topic: Divide your book into chapters based on distinct themes or topics. This helps create a logical and logical progression of ideas. Each chapter should cover a specific part or subtopic, making sure readers can easily follow along and grasp the main points being presented.

Maintain a coherent flow: Ensure that each chapter flows smoothly from one to the next. Connect the ideas and ideas discussed in the previous chapter to those in the following one. This coherence lets readers easily transition and understand how each section fits into the larger narrative.

Use transitional elements: Utilize transitional elements such as subheadings, bullet points, or summary paragraphs to guide readers through different sections within a chapter. These elements act as signposts, providing a clear roadmap of what lies ahead and helping readers navigate through complex content.

Vary the content: Mix up the types of content within your chapters and sections to keep readers engaged. Incorporate anecdotes, case studies, quotes, or illustrations to create a more dynamic reading experience. This variety prevents readers from growing bored or feeling overwhelmed by a monotonous flow of information.

Consider reader comprehension: Gauge the complexity of your content and adjust the length and structure of your chapters and sections. If your book deals with intricate ideas, breaking them down into smaller, more manageable sections can enhance readers' understanding and prevent them from feeling overwhelmed.

Seek feedback: Once you've structured your book into chapters and sections, consider seeking feedback from beta readers or editors. Their fresh perspective can provide valuable insights into whether the flow is balancing well and identify any areas that may benefit from restructuring or further attention.

By carefully balancing the length, theme, flow, and content of your book's chapters and sections, you can provide readers with a smooth and engaging reading experience. Remember to consider your audience, the complexity of your content, and seek feedback to make sure your book maintains a balanced and enjoyable narrative.

PRACTICAL TIPS ON TRANSITIONING SMOOTHLY:

Transitioning smoothly between chapters and sections is crucial in creating a seamless reading experience for your audience. It helps maintain their interest, enhances comprehension, and develops a sense of continuity throughout your book. To achieve this, here are practical tips on effectively transitioning between chapters and sections:

Preview the upcoming content: Start your chapter or section with a brief preview or summary of what the readers can expect. This creates anticipation, prepares them for the shift in topic or perspective, and keeps them connected to the overall narrative.

Recap the previous chapter: Beginning each new chapter with a concise recap of the key points or events from the previous one refreshes the reader's memory and reinforces the connection between chapters. However, ensure this recap is not excessive or repetitive, as it may discourage readers from following the book closely.

Use transitional phrases or sentences: using transitional phrases or sentences can seamlessly guide your readers from one chapter or section to another. Phrases like "In the next chapter," "Moving forward," or "Now, let's explore" provide clear signals that a transition is occurring. These transitions act as signposts, letting readers navigate through the book with ease.

Provide context: When starting a new chapter or section, provide enough context to help readers understand the setting, time frame, or any other relevant background information. This establishes a smooth transition by grounding readers in the new segment and avoiding confusion as they progress through your book.

Establish thematic connections: Spotlighting thematic connections between chapters or sections strengthens the sense of continuity and ensures a coherent reading experience. This can be done by highlighting common threads, related ideas, or recurring motifs that tie the chapters together. By doing so, you emphasize the interconnectedness of the book and deepen readers' engagement.

Create a logical flow: Ensure that the progression from one chapter or section to the next is logical and flows naturally. Avoid abrupt shifts or disjointed transitions that might disrupt your readers' comprehension. Arrange your chapters or sections in a cohesive order that offers a smooth and coherent development of ideas, events, or characters.

Use formatting or design cues: Utilize visual cues, such as section dividers, chapter numbers, or headings, to visually reinforce the transition points. This helps readers recognize the shift and mentally prepare for the upcoming content. Consistent formatting also enhances readability and reinforces the book's cohesion.

Consider pacing and structure: Pay attention to the pacing and structure of your book. While some chapters or sections may demand a slower, more reflective pace, others may require a faster rhythm or action-packed tone. Varying the pacing can maintain reader interest and make each transition feel purposeful and engaging.

Remember, the goal is to guide your readers smoothly between chapters and sections, keeping their attention and enhancing their understanding of your book's content. By offering clear previews, recaps, transitions, context, thematic connections, logical flow, formatting cues, and considering pacing and structure, you can effectively transition between chapters, providing your readers with a seamless reading experience.

USING HOOKS & CLIFFHANGERS THAT LEAVE READERS WANTING MORE:

Hooks and cliffhangers are essential tools in a writer's arsenal when keeping readers engrossed in a story. They create a sense of curiosity and anticipation, making readers eager to continue reading. In this section, we will explore various techniques that use hooks and cliffhangers to their fullest potential, ensuring readers stay hooked until the very end.

Captivating Chapter Openings:

The beginning of a chapter is a crucial moment to grab readers' attention. Starting with a memorable line or an intriguing scenario can immediately captivate readers and make them curious about what will happen next. For example:

- "The night was silent, except for the faint sound of footsteps approaching from behind."

- "The old house on the hill had always been rumored to be haunted, but tonight, the rumors were proven true."

Thought-Provoking Questions:

Posing thought-provoking questions can engage readers' curiosity and make them question the outcome of the story. These questions can be sprinkled throughout the narrative or used at strategic points to leave readers pondering. They create a desire for answers and an urge to keep reading. For instance:

- "What would you do if you discovered a hidden treasure map?"

- "How far would you go to protect your loved ones from the darkness?"

Suspenseful Endings:

Ending chapters or sections with suspense is a surefire way to make readers yearn for more. By leaving certain plot points unresolved or introducing unexpected twists, readers are left hanging, desperate to discover what will happen next. Here are a few examples:

- "As the car skidded toward the edge of the cliff, John desperately tried to grab the steering wheel, but it was too late."

- "Just as she opened the door, a blood-curdling scream echoed from the other side."

Unresolved Mysteries:

Introducing mysteries that carry throughout the story creates a sense of intrigue and mystery. By withholding information or offering only partial explanations, readers are enticed to continue reading to uncover the truth. This technique keeps them engaged, wanting to satiate their curiosity. For example:

- "The locked box in the attic held a secret that would change Sarah's life forever. But what was inside?"

- "Detective Smith stumbled upon a cryptic note at the crime scene, but deciphering its hidden message would be the key to solving the case."

Emotional Cliffhangers:

Tugging at readers' emotions can also be a powerful way to create cliffhangers. This can involve ending chapters on an emotional high or low, leaving readers desperate to know the resolution. For instance:

- "Tears streamed down her face as she read the letter, realizing she had lost everything she held dear."

- "Their lips met, sealing the promise of a new beginning. Little did they know, their happiness would be short-lived."

Foreshadowing:

Building up anticipation through foreshadowing can keep readers hooked, expecting what lies ahead. By hinting at future events without revealing the full details, readers are driven to continue reading to discover the significance of these clues. For example:

- "Little did she know, this seemingly ordinary day would soon become a turning point in her life."

-"A sense of unease filled the air, foreboding an imminent storm that would change everything."

Incorporating these techniques into your storytelling can work wonders in keeping readers eager to continue reading. By using captivating chapter openings, thought-provoking questions, suspenseful endings, unresolved mysteries, emotional cliffhangers, and strategic foreshadowing, you can create a compelling narrative that leaves readers desperately wanting more.

THE IMPORTANCE OF REGULARLY REVIEWING AND REFINING THE OUTLINE:

Regularly reviewing and refining the outline is an essential part of the writing process, as it allows for necessary changes to adapt to any changes in ideas, themes, or content. As we delve deeper into the writing process, new thoughts may emerge, old ideas may evolve, and the overall direction of the piece may shift. By frequently revisiting and reassessing our outline, we can make sure our writing remains coherent, focused, and reflects our current understanding and intentions.

One of the primary reasons for reviewing and refining the outline is to maintain alignment between the initial plan and the evolving content. As we generate ideas, conduct further research, or gain new insights, we may discover that certain sections of the outline need to be expanded, reorganized, or even discarded altogether. By consistently reviewing the outline, we can identify these necessary changes and make them before they become major roadblocks. This proactive approach saves time, prevents writer's block, and allows for a smoother writing process overall.

Reviewing the outline helps us recognize any gaps or missing connections in our work. As we refine our ideas and content, we may realize that certain points need more elaboration or clarification. By spotting these gaps early on, we can address them promptly and make sure our writing remains comprehensive and coherent. Additionally, reviewing the outline lets us identify any redundant or repetitive sections that could be eliminated or consolidated for better flow and efficiency.

Another benefit of regularly reviewing and refining the outline is that it keeps us focused on the original purpose and main message of our writing. It is easy to get lost in the intricate details and lose sight of the bigger picture. By revisiting our outline, we can assess if our writing aligns with our intended goals. This makes sure we stay on track and avoid deviating from the central theme or idea.

Regularly reviewing and refining the outline is a crucial step in the writing process. It lets us adapt to changes in ideas, themes, or content while maintaining coherence and focus. By closely examining the outline, we can make necessary changes, identify gaps or redundancies, and stay aligned with our writing goals. Ultimately, this practice enhances the overall quality of our work and contributes to a smoother and more successful writing experience.

Chapter Summary:

Chapter 5 was a real eye-opener for anyone looking to write a book. It's all about "Creating A Strong Outline" and why that's like the backbone of your whole project.

You wouldn't build a house without a plan, right? Same goes for writing a book. You've got to know where you're going before you even start. Some people think they can just wing it, but this chapter showed that's a big mistake if you want to make something folks will enjoy from the first page to the last.

The outline's your roadmap. It keeps you on track, so there's no bumps or wrong turns. It helps you put together a story that's a joy to read and makes sense to boot.

But an outline's not just about keeping things neat and tidy. It's also how you keep readers on the edge of their seats. You plan out those twists and surprises, so your story stays fresh and exciting. If you miss this step, you risk boring your readers, and that's a no-go.

Characters matter too, and an outline helps you dig into who they are and what makes them tick. You sketch them out in advance, so they come to life on the page. Readers want to feel something for the people in your book, and an outline helps make sure that happens.

And let's not forget about those big themes you want to explore. Whether it's love or politics or whatever, you've got to figure that out in your outline, or you'll end up with a jumble.

The logical flow of your book, that's another thing this chapter hammered home. If your story doesn't flow right, you'll lose your readers for sure. You've got to keep things moving smoothly from start to finish.

So, to wrap it up, Chapter 5 taught us the real deal about outlining your book. It's more than just a boring step you've got to take; it's the key to writing something that's worth reading. From your story to your characters to the big ideas you want to share, the outline's where it all comes together. Don't skip it if you want to write something great!

In our Next Chapter...

Chapter 6 - Writing Engaging Introductions: Techniques for Hooking Readers from The Beginning & Establishing the Book's Purpose

Interested in crafting the perfect start to a story? Want to know the techniques that capture readers' attention from the very first sentence? Chapter 6 offers valuable insights into the art of creating engaging beginnings.

Consider the importance of an opening sentence that instantly grabs the reader's attention. This chapter explores how to construct that critical first line, making sure readers want to continue.

Picture yourself gathered around a campfire, listening to a wise storyteller spinning a tale. With just a single sentence, you are captivated.

Your curiosity is piqued, and you yearn to know more. That is the power of a captivating opening sentence, and in this chapter, we will delve deep into its magic.

But wait, that's just the beginning. We will also explore the art of story-telling, taking inspiration from our friend Eldron, who could ignite an adventure with his words. Discover how to ignite the imagination and establish a connection with your readers - all of this awaits you here. Have you ever come across a question so thrilling that it lingers in your mind?

Thought-provoking questions can truly transform your introduction into an irresistible invitation. And let's not even begin discussing the art of painting vivid pictures with words, evoking sensations of sand between one's toes or the cry of seagulls.

Have you ever been captivated by the harmonious union of two seem-ingly incompatible elements? That is the magic of contradictions, and we will explore how to harness this charm to your advantage. This chapter is akin to a treasure chest overflowing with techniques to make your introduction engaging, mysterious, vivid, and brimming with surprises.

Chapter 6 is a comprehensive guide to the tools and techniques that can make your introduction engaging, clear, and compelling. It's designed to help you hook your readers from the first word and set the stage for the rest of your work. If you aim to enhance your writing and make your introductions stand out, this chapter has the guidance you need. Start this enlightening journey today and explore the possibilities that await you!

CHAPTER SIX

WRITING ENGAGING INTRODUCTIONS: TECHNIQUES FOR HOOKING READERS FROM THE BEGINNING & ESTABLISHING THE BOOK'S PURPOSE

THE POWER OF A CAPTIVATING OPENING SENTENCE:

THE POWER of a captivating opening sentence lies in its ability to instantly ignite curiosity, drawing readers into a world they never knew they yearned for, leaving them no choice but to be entwined in the spellbinding narrative that awaits them.

USING STORYTELLING TECHNIQUES TO CAPTIVATE READERS' INTEREST FROM THE BEGINNING:

THE ENIGMATIC ADVENTURE OF THE ANCIENT SCROLL:

Once upon a time, in a remote village nestled deep within a dense forest, there lived a wise old storyteller named Eldron. Eldron possessed an extraordinary gift - the ability to captivate his audience with his enchanting tales. As the sun set behind the tall hills, children and adults would gather around the ancient storytelling tree, eagerly awaiting Eldron's next mesmerizing narrative.

Anecdotes that Spark Imagination:

Eldron begins his tale one evening by recounting a peculiar incident from his childhood. He describes stumbling upon a mysterious map hidden inside the dusty attic of his family's cottage. The map, believed to lead to a hidden treasure, ignited young Eldron's adventurous spirit and set his heart ablaze with curiosity. This captivating anecdote not only engages the readers but also entices them to imagine the very treasure and wonder what happened next.

Relatable Experiences to Establish Connection:

Eldron beautifully weaves his narratives with relatable experiences that tug at the readers' heartstrings. In his next story, he describes the struggles of a young girl named Lily, who lives in a bustling city and yearns for a connection with nature. Eldron's vivid descriptions of Lily's longing for the tranquility of the village, where people live in harmony with nature, and his depiction of her journey to find solace, establish an emotional connection with readers seeking solace in their own lives.

Suspense-building Techniques to Trigger Curiosity:

As Eldron dives deeper into his tales, he skillfully uses suspense-building techniques to keep readers on the edge of their seats. In one gripping story, Eldron unveils an ancient scroll hidden deep within a hidden cave. The scroll, he explains with a mischievous glimmer in his eye, holds an encrypted secret that, if deciphered, could wield immense power. With every word, Eldron masterfully unveils clues, leaving readers yearning to unravel the mystery alongside the protagonist.

By employing storytelling techniques like anecdotes, relatable experiences, and suspense-building, Eldron effortlessly captivates his audience from the beginning. His skillful storytelling brings imagination to life, cultivates an emotional bond, and triggers curiosity, leaving his readers longing for more. Eldron's mesmerizing narratives continue to transport his listeners to ethereal realms and inspire them to forge their own remarkable stories.

CREATING INTRIGUE WITH A THOUGHT-PROVOKING QUESTION:

Introductions play a crucial role in captivating readers and setting the tone for the entire book. They serve as gateways to new ideas and fresh perspectives. But what if I told you that there's an art to crafting thought-provoking questions that spark intrigue and leave readers craving answers? Picture this: a question so compelling that it tickles your curiosity, dances on the edge of your mind, and keeps you engaged until the last page. Are you ready to unlock the secrets of posing these intriguing questions, transforming your introduction into an irresistible invitation to discover more?

SETTING THE STAGE: THE IMPORTANCE OF PROVIDING CONTEXT AND ESTABLISHING THE BOOK'S PURPOSE.

When starting a book, it is essential to set the stage by providing context and establishing the book's purpose. This first step is crucial as it helps orient readers and gives them a clear understanding of what they can expect from the content that follows. By providing context, authors can create a foundation on which readers can build their knowledge and understanding.

Context is the backdrop against which the book's purpose unfolds. It can include historical, cultural, or societal circumstances relevant to the topic. For example, if the book is a historical novel set during World War II, providing context about the war's causes, major events, and the impact on people's lives can help readers better grasp the story's significance.

Establishing the book's purpose is equally important. This involves clarifying the author's intentions, or goals for writing the book. It answers the reader's question of why this book exists and what benefit they can derive from reading it. The purpose could be to educate, entertain, inspire, challenge, or simply provide enjoyment.

By clearly stating the purpose, readers will have realistic expectations of the content. For example, if the purpose of a self-help book is to provide practical steps for personal growth, the reader knows to expect advice, exercises, and strategies. But if the purpose is to explore the complexities of human relationships through fictional characters, the reader expects a narrative that delves into emotions and experiences.

Providing context and establishing the book's purpose also helps readers connect with the author and develop trust. When readers understand the context, they can relate to the story more effectively. When they know the purpose, they are more likely to engage with the content, knowing it aligns with their own goals or interests.

In addition, orienting readers from the beginning helps them navigate the book more easily. They gain a clear understanding of the book's scope, structure, and organization. This enables them to expect and follow the flow of ideas and concepts presented throughout the book, enhancing their overall reading experience.

Setting the stage by providing context and establishing the book's purpose is an essential step in creating a meaningful connection with readers. It lets them approach the content with the right mindset, aligning their expectations and enabling them to immerse themselves in the book's message. When readers clearly understand what they can expect, they are more likely to engage with the content and derive greater value from the reading experience.

USING DESCRIPTIVE LANGUAGE & IMAGERY TO PAINT VIVID PICTURES IN READERS' MINDS:

Imagine standing on a secluded white sandy beach, the warm sun rays gently kissing your skin. The salty ocean breeze rustles through the towering palm trees that line the shore, their lush green fronds swaying in perfect harmony. As you walk toward the water, you feel the fine grains of sand, like soft silk, slipping through your toes. The crystal-clear turquoise waves crash against the shoreline, forming frothy cascades that sparkle under the brilliant sunshine. Above, seagulls gracefully glide across the endless blue canvas of the sky, their ethereal calls echoing in the distance. In this idyllic setting, nature's symphony plays out, coaxing every sense to awaken and surrender to its tranquil embrace.

GENERATING INTRIGUE THROUGH CONTRADICTION:

In the vast universe of writing, one technique that captivates readers like no other is the art of generating intrigue through contradiction. It is a mesmerizing dance of juxtaposing ideas or statements in introductions to create a sense of tension and curiosity. This unique approach tantalizes the mind, urging readers to delve deeper into the text to unravel the hidden truths and comprehend the underlying ideas.

Contradiction is a powerful tool that defies conventional logic and challenges our preconceived notions. By presenting seemingly conflicting ideas side by side, writers can astound and bewilder their audience in the blink of an eye. The clash of ideas creates friction, sparking a fire of curiosity within readers' hearts, demanding them to question and explore further.

Consider an introduction that starts with a line like, "Love and chaos danced gracefully in his heart." The contradiction within this statement immediately piques curiosity. How can love and chaos coexist harmoniously? What does this seemingly contradictory combination say about the protagonist's emotions or the story's central theme?

By leveraging contrasting ideas or statements in introductions, writers not only leave readers intrigued but also ignite their curiosity to comprehend both sides of the paradox. It's as if they hold a key to a secret door, enticing readers to venture inside and unlock the mysteries lurking within.

Contradiction stimulates critical thinking. When confronted with contrasting ideas, readers are compelled to analyze and synthesize the information presented to make sense of the apparent contradiction. This mental exercise fuels the desire to explore further, as readers yearn to understand how these conflicting elements come together to form a cohesive narrative.

Applying this technique is not limited to any specific genre or subject matter. From thought-provoking essays to perplexing mystery novels or even mind-bending science fiction, using contrasting ideas in introductions can enthrall audiences across a wide range of literary landscapes.

Generating intrigue through contradiction is a captivating strategy that triggers tension, curiosity, and the innate human desire to explore the unknown. By juxtaposing contrasting ideas or statements in introductions, writers weave a spell so alluring that readers inevitably embark on a quest for deeper understanding. So, dear reader, let the power of contradiction enthrall you, and journey forth into the realm of literature's most enigmatic and captivating tales.

EXPERIMENTING WITH DIFFERENT INTRODUCTION STYLES:

Introduction styles play a crucial role in capturing the attention of your audience and setting the tone for the rest of your message. Whether you're writing an essay, delivering a speech, or crafting a marketing campaign, the introduction is your opportunity to make a memorable first impression.

But which approach is the most effective? Is it starting with a provocative statement that grabs attention? Or perhaps a surprising fact that piques curiosity? Maybe a strong emotional appeal that resonates deeply with your audience? In this experiment, we will explore different introduction styles to gain insights into their impact and discover the most effective method for engaging your specific target audience.

By stepping outside the conventional norms and thinking creatively, this experiment aims to unlock the secrets behind captivating introductions and enhance your communication skills. So, let's embark on this journey of experimentation and innovation to create introductions that leave a lasting impression on your audience.

Chapter Summary:

Chapter 6 - "Writing Engaging Introductions: Techniques for Hooking Readers from The Beginning & Establishing the Book's Purpose" teaches you the secrets of grabbing your readers' attention right from the start. Think about it like casting a magic spell. If you want to pull them into your world, you've got to do it from the first sentence.

Imagine a wise old storyteller, Eldron, enchanting folks with his tales. He doesn't just start talking about random stuff; he opens with something that'll get their hearts racing, something that'll make them lean in and listen. This chapter's going to teach you how to do that with your writing.

First, we looked at how a strong opening sentence can catch readers, like hooking a big fish. It's got to ignite curiosity, making them think, "What's this about?" and keep reading.

Then, we dove into storytelling techniques, like Eldron's tales. He used anecdotes that spark imagination, relatable experiences to connect, and suspense-building to make readers bite their nails. Your writing's got to do the same if you want to keep folks turning those pages.

We also talked about asking thought-provoking questions. It's like dangling a carrot in front of your readers, making them want to chase after it until they get to the end.

Next, we touched on the importance of setting the stage. You've got to let readers know what they're in for. Give them the context and lay out what your book's all about. It's like giving them a map so they don't get lost along the way.

We looked at using descriptive language to paint pictures in readers' minds. Make them see the beach, feel the breeze, hear the waves. Your words have to make it real for them.

Then, we explored generating intrigue through contradiction. It's like mixing two colors you never thought would go together but somehow make something beautiful. Contradiction makes readers stop and think, and that's what you want.

Lastly, we played with different introduction styles. It's like trying on different outfits to see what fits best. There's no one-size-fits-all, so you've got to experiment to find what works for your audience.

So, that's what Chapter 6 is all about. To draw readers in, make them feel, think, and yearn for more, you've got to master the art of the engaging introduction. It's not just about writing; it's about creating a doorway into another world, and this chapter's going to show you how to make that doorway irresistible.

In our Next Chapter...

Curious about the art of influence?

Chapter 7 offers a comprehensive guide. It's about more than just convincing talk; it's about connecting with people and resonating with what matters to them.

First, the chapter demystifies what persuasion entails. It's not merely about words but incorporating visuals like pictures and graphs. These techniques can be applied in various settings, whether professionally or among friends.

These invaluable skills can be applied not only in your professional life but also in conversations with friends.

However, before you embark on your persuasive journey, it's crucial to understand your audience. What are their interests? What are their needs? Conducting social media research or other forms of investigation can help you fathom their desires, letting you strike a chord that resonates deeply.

Now, let's delve into the exciting part. You will discover how to construct an argument that demands attention. Compelling evidence, critical thinking, and the ability to stir hearts are essential. Yet, it's vital to articulate your ideas, ensuring comprehension by all.

So, what's the significance of Chapter 7? It equips you with a comprehensive toolkit to captivate your audience. You will learn to wield language, visuals, and even videos to articulate your point effectively. Honesty, respect, and coherence are paramount.

Whether talking to a crowd or engaging with a solitary individual, this chapter empowers you to master the art of persuasion—a formidable skill that empowers you to effect change through the power of words. If this resonates with you, immerse yourself in Chapter 7.

It transcends mere rhetoric; it fosters genuine connections.

MASTERING THE ART OF PERSUASION: TOOLS & TECHNIQUES FOR PRESENTING YOUR IDEAS PERSUASIVELY TO INFLUENCE READERS

INTRODUCTION TO THE ART OF PERSUASION:

COMMUNICATION IS a fundamental part of human interaction. Whether it is a simple conversation or a formal presentation, the main goal of communication is to convey a message and, more important, to make sure the audience understands, accepts, and acts on that message. This is where the art of persuasion comes into play.

Persuasion is the ability to influence others through effective communication. It is a powerful tool that can shape opinions, change behaviors, and ultimately achieve desired outcomes. In today's world, where information is abundant and attention spans are limited, the art of persuasion has become more essential than ever before.

Effective persuasion involves several key elements. First, it requires a comprehensive understanding of the target audience, including their needs, concerns, and values. By appealing to these factors, persuaders can connect with their audience on a deeper level, establishing trust and credibility.

Second, effective persuasion relies on compelling arguments and evidence. Persuaders must provide well-structured and logical reasoning, supported by facts, statistics, and expert opinions. This helps to build a strong case for their message, making it difficult for the audience to refute or ignore.

Additionally, the art of persuasion also encompasses the skill of emotional appeal. Humans are inherently emotional creatures, and our decisions are often driven by our feelings. By appealing to the emotions of their audience, persuaders can create a strong connection and motivate them to act.

Persuasion is not limited to verbal communication alone. Visual aids, such as graphs, charts, and images, can enhance the persuasiveness of a message. They can simplify complex information, make data more real, and leave a lasting impression on the audience.

The impact of persuasion is far-reaching. In the business world, persuasion is essential for salespeople, managers, and leaders, as they seek to convince customers, employees, and stakeholders about the benefits of their products, ideas, or strategies. In politics, persuasion plays a crucial role in winning elections and gaining public support for policies and initiatives. Even in personal relationships, persuasion helps individuals to express their thoughts, negotiate, and resolve conflicts.

Persuasion is an art form that involves understanding, connecting with, and influencing an audience. Through effective communication techniques, including emotional appeal, logical arguments, and visual aids, persuaders can achieve their desired outcomes. The art of persuasion is not limited to a specific domain but is essential in all parts of life. By mastering this skill, individuals can effectively communicate, influence others, and bring about positive change.

TECHNIQUES FOR ANALYZING & UNDERSTANDING YOUR TARGET AUDIENCE:

Understanding your audience is a crucial step in developing effective persuasive arguments. By analyzing and understanding your target audience, including their needs, preferences, and beliefs, you can tailor your arguments to resonate with them. Here are techniques to help you gain deeper insights into your audience and create persuasive arguments that effectively address their concerns:

Research your audience: Start by researching and gathering data about your target audience. This can include demographic information such as age, gender, location, and education level. Additionally, psychographic information, such as their values, interests, and lifestyle, is also essential. Use various research methods such as surveys, interviews, or data analytics to gather relevant information.

Create buyer personas: Once you have collected data, create buyer personas. These are fictional representations of your target audience that encompass their features, preferences, motivations, and challenges. Develop multiple buyer personas representing different segments of your audience to better understand their unique needs.

Conduct interviews or surveys: To gain deeper insights, engage with your target audience directly. Conduct interviews or surveys to ask specific questions about their preferences, needs, and beliefs. Engaging with your audience will provide qualitative data that enhances your understanding of their mindset.

Analyze social media and online discussions: Monitor social media platforms and online forums relevant to your audience. Observe their conversations, comments, and posts to gain insights into their interests, concerns, and existing opinions. Analyzing these discussions can help you identify common pain points and tailor your persuasive arguments.

Review competitor strategies: Study how your competitors are targeting the same audience. Analyze their messaging, content, and communication strategies. Identify the gaps and opportunities you can leverage to differentiate your persuasive arguments effectively.

Identify needs, preferences, and pain points: Based on your research, identify the key needs, preferences, and pain points of your target audience. Understanding what motivates them, what they care about, and the challenges they face will let you direct your persuasive arguments toward addressing these specific areas.

Consider different communication channels: Analyze where your target audience is most active and receptive. Are they more engaged on social media platforms, forums, or industry-specific publications? Tailor your persuasive arguments according to the preferred communication channels of your audience to maximize their reach and impact.

Test and iterate: Once you have tailored your persuasive arguments, test them with a small segment of your target audience. Collect feedback, analyze the response, and refine your arguments as needed. Continuously iterate and improve your messaging to ensure it aligns with the evolving needs and preferences of your audience.

By using these techniques and understanding your target audience, you can tailor your persuasive arguments effectively, resonating with their needs, preferences, and beliefs. When you speak directly to the concerns and desires of your audience, your persuasive arguments become more compelling and influential, leading to better engagement and desired outcomes.

Crafting a compelling argument is a crucial skill that can be applied in various parts of life, including academics, professional settings, and personal interactions. To build a strong and persuasive argument, one must use a combination of evidence, logical reasoning, and emotional appeal. This guide aims to provide strategies for constructing persuasive arguments by avoiding common pitfalls and fallacies.

Begin with Strong Evidence:

To strengthen an argument, it is crucial to start with strong evidence that supports your claims. This evidence can include factual data, expert opinions, research studies, or historical examples. Credible sources lend credibility to your argument and show it is grounded in well-established information.

Use Logical Reasoning:

Logical reasoning is the backbone of a compelling argument. Deductive reasoning, which involves moving from general principles to specific conclusions, and inductive reasoning, which involves drawing general conclusions based on specific evidence, should be employed effectively. Present clear and logical connections between your premises and your conclusion to make your argument persuasive.

Appeal to Emotions Appropriately:

While evidence and logical reasoning form the foundation of a strong argument, incorporating emotional appeal can further enhance its persuasive power. By connecting to the emotions of your audience, you can engage them on a deeper level, making them more receptive to your argument. Storytelling, personal anecdotes, and relatable examples can be powerful tools in eliciting emotional responses.

Consider Counterarguments:

To strengthen your own argument, it is essential to expect and address potential counterarguments. Acknowledging opposing viewpoints shows your awareness and understanding of the complexity of the topic. By presenting and refuting counterarguments, you establish the credibility of your own stance and showcase your ability to critically evaluate different perspectives.

Avoid Common Pitfalls and Fallacies:

A strong argument relies on avoiding common pitfalls and fallacies, which can weaken your position and compromise your credibility. Examples of fallacies include ad hominem attacks (attacking the person instead of the argument), straw man fallacy (misrepresenting your opponent's position), and appeal to authority (relying only on the opinion of an authority figure). Carefully evaluate your argument for logical consistency and steer clear of these logical fallacies.

Maintain Clarity and Conciseness:

To make your argument more compelling, it is crucial to communicate your ideas, concisely, and effectively. Avoid using complex jargon or convoluted sentences that may confuse or alienate your audience. Use concise and straightforward language to make sure your argument is accessible and easily understandable to a wide range of individuals.

Building a strong and persuasive argument requires a careful balance of evidence, logical reasoning, and emotional appeal. By incorporating these strategies into your argumentative endeavors, you can construct compelling narratives that sway opinions and foster meaningful discussions. Being mindful of common pitfalls and fallacies will further enhance the strength and credibility of your argument. With practice and dedication, you can become a master at crafting compelling arguments that leave a lasting impact.

USING LANGUAGE AND RHETORICAL DEVICES TO CAPTIVATE READERS' ATTENTION & SWAY THEIR OPINIONS:

In the realm of communication, language holds immense power - the power to inspire, motivate, and even persuade. This captivating force lies in the strategic use of rhetorical devices, persuasive language techniques, and vivid imagery. The art of persuasion encompasses the ability to captivate readers' attention, immerse them in a whirlpool of emotions, and ultimately sway their opinions. By deconstructing the elements that make language impactful, we can uncover its true potential in the realm of persuasion.

Creating Vivid Imagery:

One of the most effective ways to engage readers and elicit an emotional response is through the usage of vivid imagery. By carefully selecting and arranging words, an author can paint a picture so vivid that readers can almost see, taste, and feel what is being described. Vivid imagery lets the audience directly experience the message and fosters a deep connection between the writer and the reader. By appealing to the senses, persuasion becomes more than just words on a page; it transforms into an immersive experience.

Rhetorical Devices: Metaphors and Analogies:

Metaphors and analogies are powerful tools in persuasion that let writers draw parallels between different ideas or objects, enabling readers to grasp complex ideas more easily. Metaphors infuse language with emotional significance, making messages more relatable and relaying information in a memorable way. Analogies, on the other hand, create comparisons, aiding readers in understanding a new idea by relating it to something familiar. By harnessing metaphors and analogies, writers can succinctly convey complex ideas and create lasting impact.

Harnessing Persuasive Language Techniques:

Persuasive language techniques are used to influence readers' thoughts and beliefs, compelling them to align with the author's perspective. With powerful techniques such as rhetorical questions, emotional appeals, and the use of inclusive language, writers can manipulate the reader's emotions and rationality, nudging them toward the intended persuasion. These techniques add credibility, urgency, and a personal touch to the words, enhancing the overall persuasiveness of the message.

Language has an inherent power to persuade, and through vivid imagery, metaphors and analogies, as well as persuasive language techniques, writers can effectively captivate readers and sway their opinions. The art of persuasion lies not only in providing logical arguments, but also in connecting with readers on an emotional level. By using rhetorical devices, authors can transcend the limitations of words, inspiring readers to see the world from a new perspective. In the realm of persuasion, language is the key that unlocks minds, hearts, and ultimately, the desired change.

STRUCTURING YOUR IDEAS TO GUIDE READERS THROUGH YOUR ARGUMENTS SEAMLESSLY:

The introduction plays a crucial role in persuading readers to continue reading your piece and consider your arguments. Here are tips to make your introduction effective:

Grab attention: Start with a compelling hook, such as a thought-provoking question, an interesting fact, or a relevant anecdote that relates to your topic. This will engage readers from the beginning.

Present the thesis statement: Clearly state your main argument or position in a concise and strong thesis statement. This will guide readers and make it easier for them to follow your arguments.

Transitions:

Transitions are vital for maintaining the flow of your ideas and guiding readers through your arguments seamlessly. Here are strategies to use transitions effectively:

Use transitional words: Words like "however," "therefore," "in addition," or "on the contrary" help create a smooth transition between paragraphs or ideas. These words connect thoughts and show the logical progression of your arguments.

Repeat and rephrase: Utilize repetition and rephrasing to reinforce key concepts or ideas. This makes sure readers understand your points and can easily follow the overall structure of your piece.

The conclusion is your opportunity to leave a lasting impact on readers and solidify your persuasive argument. Here's how to write a strong conclusion:

Summarize your main points: Briefly recap the main arguments or evidence you presented throughout your piece. This reminds readers of your key points and reinforces your main thesis.

Restate the thesis: Rephrase your thesis statement in a fresh and impactful way. However, avoid simply copying your original thesis; instead, add a sense of closure by emphasizing the importance of your argument and its implications.

Call-to-action: If appropriate, end your conclusion with a call-to-action. Encourage readers to act based on your argument, whether it's supporting a cause, changing a behavior, or further investigating the topic.

By using these tips for organizing and structuring your ideas, you can make your persuasive writing more compelling and persuasive. Remember to start with a strong introduction, use effective transitions, and end with a memorable conclusion. With these strategies, you can guide readers seamlessly through your arguments, increasing the persuasive impact of your writing.

ENGAGING VISUALS AND MULTIMEDIA: ENHANCING THE PERSUASIVE POWER OF YOUR IDEAS

In today's world, where attention spans are becoming shorter and information overload is a constant challenge, the power of visuals and multimedia elements cannot be underestimated. Whether you are presenting your ideas in a business meeting, a conference, or a class-room, incorporating engaging visuals can significantly enhance the persuasive impact of your message. This article explores the impact of visuals, such as charts, graphs, and multimedia elements, and provides guidelines for their proper integration and presentation.

Capture Attention:

Visuals can immediately capture the audience's attention. Use eye-catching and relevant visuals to draw your audience in and create an initial impact. This could be in the form of a striking image, a well-designed chart, or an intriguing multimedia element.

Enhance Understanding:

Visuals are effective in conveying complex information in a concise and understandable manner. Use charts and graphs to present data and statistics in a way easy to interpret. Exploring visual metaphors can also help to simplify abstract ideas and make them more relatable.

Help with Memory Retention:

Research has shown that combining visual elements with textual information enhances memory retention. Incorporate visuals that align with your message, as this can greatly contribute to your audience's ability to remember and recall your ideas long after the presentation.

Create Emotional Impact:

Visuals have the power to evoke emotions and create a deeper connection with your audience. Use multimedia elements, such as videos or images, to tell stories or share examples that elicit emotions related to your ideas. This emotional impact can reinforce your persuasive message and leave a lasting impression.

Maintain Consistency and Clarity:

When integrating visuals and multimedia elements, ensure they align with your overall message and reinforce key points. Avoid clutter or irrelevant material that may confuse your audience. Strive for a clean, well-organized layout that allows your visuals to be easily understood and appreciated.

Practice Proper Integration:

Integrating visuals and multimedia elements seamlessly during your presentation is crucial. Familiarize yourself with the software or tools you will be using to present your visuals, ensuring they are easily accessible and properly displayed. Practice transitioning between visuals and your spoken content, so you can deliver a smooth and coherent presentation.

Remember that visuals and multimedia elements should supplement your ideas, not overshadow them. They support and amplify your message, rather than replace it. Keep your visuals concise, relevant, and visually appealing to maintain your audience's attention and effectively convey your persuasive ideas.

Incorporating engaging visuals and multimedia elements into your presentations is a powerful tool in enhancing the persuasive power of your ideas. Embrace the potential of visuals to captivate your audience, enhance understanding, help with memory retention, create emotional impact, and maintain clarity. With proper integration and presentation, visuals can significantly elevate the effectiveness of your message and leave a lasting impact on your audience.

ETHICAL CONSIDERATIONS & BUILDING TRUST WITH YOUR AUDIENCE:

Ethical Considerations:

When engaging in persuasive communication, it is crucial to consider the ethical dimensions of your message. Persuasion should always be grounded in transparency, honesty, and respect for the autonomy of your readers. Failure to adhere to these ethical principles can lead to a loss of credibility and trust, ultimately undermining your persuasive efforts. Here are key considerations for ensuring ethical persuasion:

Transparency: Be clear about your intentions and reveal any potential conflicts of interest. Your readers deserve to know if you have any personal or financial stakes in the topic you are advocating. Transparency builds trust and shows you are genuinely interested in providing valuable information rather than manipulating others for personal gain.

Honesty: Always present accurate and reliable information. Misleading or misrepresenting facts not only compromises your integrity but also undermines the persuasiveness of your argument. Be careful in your research and fact-checking to make sure your claims are sound and supported by evidence.

Respect readers' autonomy: Recognize that your audience has the right to form their own opinions and make their own choices. Avoid using manipulative tactics that infringe upon their autonomy. Instead, present your arguments in a respectful and non-coercive manner, letting readers make informed decisions based on their own judgment.

Credibility: Maintain a strong reputation by consistently delivering reliable and well-researched content. Uphold academic or professional standards when presenting your ideas, making sure your arguments are logical, coherent, and supported by credible sources. Showing expertise, experience, and knowledge will enhance your credibility, making your persuasive efforts more impactful.

Building Trust: Establishing trust with your audience is paramount for effective persuasion. Engage in open and respectful dialogue, encouraging feedback and addressing any concerns or criticisms honestly. Actively listen to your readers and show empathy, as this fosters a connection that encourages them to be more receptive to your message.

Empower informed decision-making: Instead of seeking blind agreement or conformity, empower your audience to make informed choices. Provide them with a range of perspectives and counterarguments, showing you respect their ability to critically evaluate information and come to their own conclusions.

To summarize, ethical considerations are vital when engaging in persuasion. By embracing transparency, honesty, and respecting readers' autonomy, you can build trust and maintain credibility with your audience. Upholding these principles makes sure your persuasive efforts are based on ethics and integrity.

Engaging Visuals and Multimedia: Exploring the impact of visuals, such as charts, graphs, and multimedia elements, in enhancing the persuasive power of your ideas, along with guidelines for their proper integration and presentation.

In today's visually-oriented world, the power of visuals and multimedia cannot be overlooked regarding effective persuasion. Integrating compelling and well-crafted visuals can significantly enhance the impact of your ideas. Here are guidelines for their proper integration and presentation:

Relevance: Select visuals that are directly related to your message and help clarify complex ideas or data. Irrelevant or unrelated visuals can confuse your audience and undermine the persuasiveness of your argument.

Accuracy: Ensure that the visuals accurately represent the information they intend to convey. Misleading or manipulated visuals can damage your credibility and trust with your audience. Use reliable sources and data to create accurate visuals.

Simplicity: Avoid visual clutter and keep your visuals simple and easy to understand. Remove any unnecessary details that might distract or confuse your audience. Simplicity enhances the clarity and impact of your message.

Integration: Integrate visuals seamlessly within the flow of your persuasive piece. Avoid isolating them or presenting them as an afterthought. Incorporate visuals strategically to complement and reinforce your written content.

Variety: Utilize a range of visuals to cater to different learning styles and engage a broader audience. Incorporate charts, graphs, infographics, images, or multimedia elements to provide diverse ways for your audience to comprehend and connect with your message.

Visual appeal: Pay attention to the design and aesthetics of your visuals. Use color, typography, and layout to make your visuals visually appealing and professional. Invest in high-quality visuals that are visually engaging while maintaining clarity.

Accessibility: Consider the accessibility needs of your audience. Make sure your visuals are accessible to individuals with visual impairments by providing alternative text descriptions or audio descriptions where necessary. Additionally, provide alternative formats for individuals who may have difficulty accessing certain file types.

Visuals should enhance, not overshadow, your written content. They should support and add value to your persuasive arguments, helping your audience grasp complex ideas more easily. By following these guidelines, you can harness the persuasive power of visuals and multimedia to strengthen your overall message and engage your audience more effectively.

Chapter Summary:

Chapter 7 takes you on a journey of learning the art of persuasion. It's more than just talking; it's about connecting with people in a way that makes them understand, accept, and act on what you're saying. First up, you've got to know what persuasion is all about, and it's not just words. You can use pictures or graphs to help people see things your way.

But before you jump in, you need to understand who you're talking to. What do they like? What do they need? You must get inside their heads and figure out where they hang out online or in the real world. Once you know your audience, you can start building your argument. You need to have strong evidence, logical thinking, and touch their emotions. But be careful! Keep it clear, or you could mess things up.

This chapter hands you all the tools to get people to listen to your ideas. You'll learn how to use language, metaphors, pictures, and even videos to make people feel something. You'll learn how to set up your ideas in a way that flows and sticks in their mind. And above all, you've got to be honest and respectful.

Whether you're in business, politics, or living your everyday life, this chapter shows you how to master persuasion, and that's a big deal. If you can open up people's minds and hearts, you've got some serious power, and you can make real change happen.

In our Next Chapter…

Are you ready to explore the fascinating world of research citations? Look no further than Chapter 8.

Here's why it's must-read:

Acknowledging Intellectual Contributions: Show appreciation instead of borrowing. Citations ensure that you give credit where it's due, respecting the original thinkers and their valuable insights.

Strengthening Your Arguments: By including citations, you demonstrate thorough research, earning the respect and agreement of your audience. Your ideas become more persuasive and logical.

Displaying Expertise: Proper use of citations acts as a badge of authority, declaring, "Trust me, I know my stuff." It exhibits your command over the subject matter.

Connecting Ideas Across Disciplines: Build bridges between concepts and facilitate exploration of related works, even beyond your immediate field.

Contributing to Future Research: You can play a pivotal role in inspiring future researchers. How exciting is that?

Enhancing Your Reputation: Play fair, cite accurately, and watch as your peers tip their hats to you in admiration.

And remember, it's not just about what you cite, but how you do it. This chapter delves into the major citation styles – APA, MLA, Chicago, and IEEE – each with its own playbook. Mastering them is essential to elevate your game.

We also take a close look at in-text citations – where the artistry comes into play. Get this right, and your writing will not only stand out but also shine brightly. Let's not forget about the art of using quotes, paraphrases, and selecting reliable sources.

You must be precise and adept, skillfully blending quotes and paraphrases like a seasoned pro, while carefully choosing sources that carry weight.

If you're eager to enhance your research skills, Chapter 8 is the toolbox you've been waiting for. It's not about memorizing rules; it's about understanding the why and the how.

Consider it a roadmap that will elevate your work from good to exceptional. If you want to add a touch of authenticity to your writing, this chapter is calling your name. Let's dive in and make your work truly shine!

∿

ADDING DEPTH WITH EFFECTIVE RESEARCH CITATIONS: EXPLORING DIFFERENT CITATION STYLES & UTILIZING RESEARCH TO ADD CREDIBILITY TO YOUR WORK

UNDERSTANDING THE IMPORTANCE OF RESEARCH CITATIONS IN ACADEMIC WRITING:

IN THE REALM OF ACADEMIA, research citations hold paramount importance. They not only acknowledge the original authors' contributions but also enable readers to locate and verify sources, thus adding credibility to one's work. This chapter aims to explore the reasons why accurate and proper citation styles are crucial for enhancing the credibility of academic writing.

Providing Credit and Acknowledgment:

Research citations are essential as they provide credit and acknowledgment to the original authors whose ideas and work paved the way for subsequent research. By citing relevant sources, researchers honor intellectual property and avoid plagiarism, displaying ethical conduct in academia.

Verifying Information and Strengthening Arguments:

Citations serve as a pathway for readers to retrace the steps of earlier research to confirm and verify the information presented by the author. Including accurate citations enhances the credibility of claims and arguments made within an academic work. It shows the author has conducted a thorough literature review to support their assertions.

Demonstrating Depth of Scholarship:

Proper citation styles show a writer's depth of scholarship by showcasing their familiarity with existing research and theoretical frameworks. When the author cites a range of reputable sources, it shows a comprehensive exploration of the topic, adding weight and authority to their work.

Promoting Interdisciplinary Connections:

Citations also help with interdisciplinary connections by connecting researchers from various fields. They enable readers to explore related literature from different disciplines, fostering collaboration and exchange of ideas. Proper citations encourage interdisciplinary research by highlighting the interconnectedness of knowledge.

Helping with Future Research:

Academic work builds on previous research, and citations let future researchers trace the evolution of ideas and build on existing knowledge. A proper citation style provides a roadmap for further exploration, enabling others to investigate new parts of a particular topic or replicate and verify previous findings.

Enhancing Academic Reputation:

Maintaining accurate and proper citation styles contributes to building an author's academic reputation. Citing reputable sources and adhering to universally accepted citation formats shows scholarly competence. It also prevents accusations of intellectual theft that could tarnish an author's reputation in the academic community.

Research citations play a vital role in academic writing. Accurate and proper citation styles not only provide credit to the original authors but also enhance the credibility of scholarly work. They verify information, strengthen arguments, show scholarship depth, promote interdisciplinary connections, and help with future research. Academic writers must focus on precise and consistent citations to add credibility, foster knowledge exchange, and contribute to the advancement of their respective fields.

EXPLORING VARIOUS CITATION STYLES SUCH AS APA, MLA, CHICAGO, AND IEEE, INCLUDING THEIR SPECIFIC REQUIREMENTS & FORMATS:

Citation styles are crucial for academic writing as they provide a standardized format for acknowledging the sources used in a research paper or publication. This section aims to comprehensively explore four widely used citation styles: APA, MLA, Chicago, and IEEE. By examining their specific requirements and formats, readers will gain a solid understanding of how to properly cite sources under each style.

APA Style:

The American Psychological Association (APA) style is commonly used in social sciences, education, and psychology. It emphasizes the author-date in-text citation style and uses a references page at the end of the document. Key elements of APA style include the use of hanging indents, double-spacing, and italics for titles of books and journals.

MLA Style:

Modern Language Association (MLA) style is often used in humanities, literature, and liberal arts. It uses a parenthetical in-text citation format and includes a Works Cited page at the end. MLA style requires single-spacing, a hanging indent, and italics for book titles, while article titles are enclosed in quotation marks.

Chicago Style:

The Chicago Manual of Style is common in history, literature, and the arts. It offers two main variants: the notes and bibliography system and the author-date system. The notes and bibliography system uses footnotes or endnotes for in-text citations and includes a bibliography at the end. But the author-date system uses parenthetical citations and a detailed reference list. Chicago style requires the use of block quotes, footnotes or endnotes for more explanations, and double-spacing.

IEEE Style:

The Institute of Electrical and Electronics Engineers (IEEE) uses its own citation style predominantly in the fields of engineering, computer science, and technology. IEEE style uses a numerical in-text citation system and includes a reference list at the end. Key features of IEEE style include the use of square brackets for in-text citations, numerical superscripts, and single-spacing.

By exploring the APA, MLA, Chicago, and IEEE citation styles, this chapter has provided a comprehensive overview of their specific requirements and formats. Understanding these guidelines is crucial for researchers and students, as it lets them properly cite sources in their academic work. Whether it is APA's author-date format, MLA's parenthetical citations, Chicago's notes and bibliography system, or IEEE's numerical approach, selecting the proper citation style enhances the credibility and validity of scholarly work.

MASTERING THE ART OF IN-TEXT CITATIONS:

In academic writing, it is crucial to effectively integrate research into your writing and give credit to the original sources of ideas and information. One of the most common ways to do this is through in-text citations. Mastering the art of in-text citations is vital for any writer aiming to produce well-researched and properly attributed work.

Foremost, it is important to understand what an in-text citation is. An in-text citation is a way of acknowledging an external source within your own writing. It serves as a brief reference that directs readers to a detailed entry in the reference list or bibliography, which provides comprehensive information about the source.

To create an in-text citation, there are several citation styles to choose from, such as APA (American Psychological Association), MLA (Modern Language Association), or Chicago style. Each style has its own set of guidelines, so it is important to become familiar with the specific requirements of your chosen style.

Despite the citation style you choose, there are a few general principles to follow when using in-text citations. First, the in-text citation should typically be placed right after the information or idea from the external source. This helps readers easily identify which parts of your writing are sourced from external research. Second, the in-text citation should include the author's last name and the year of publication, which helps readers locate the full reference in the reference list or bibliography.

For example, imagine you are writing a paper on the importance of exercise in maintaining mental health. You come across a study conducted by Smith in 2018, which supports your argument. In-text citations for this source would vary based on the citation style chosen:

In APA style: "Regular exercise has been shown to significantly improve mental well-being (Smith, 2018)."

In MLA style: "According to Smith, regular exercise can have a profound impact on mental health (45)."

In Chicago style: "Smith highlights the importance of exercise for mental well-being (2018)."

Consult the specific guidelines of your chosen citation style for more in-depth examples and variations.

In addition to properly attributing ideas, in-text citations also add credibility to your writing. By incorporating well-sourced information, you show a thorough understanding of the topic and strengthen your own arguments by building on established research.

Finally, when using in-text citations, it is crucial to avoid plagiarism. Plagiarism is the act of using someone else's work or ideas without giving them credit. By properly attributing sources through in-text citations, you show academic integrity and make sure your writing is ethically sound.

Mastering the art of in-text citations requires practice and attentiveness to the specific guidelines of your chosen citation style. By effectively integrating research into your writing and properly attributing ideas and information, you can produce well-researched and credible work that contributes to the academic conversation.

INCORPORATING DIRECT QUOTES & PARAPHRASES:

When conducting research, incorporating direct quotes and paraphrases from reliable sources is an essential skill to ensure accuracy and credibility. Understanding the best practices for using these techniques appropriately is crucial. This guide will delve into the dos and don'ts of incorporating direct quotes and paraphrases, including when and how to use them effectively.

Understanding Direct Quotes:

Direct quotes involve replicating the exact words from a research source and placing them within quotation marks. This technique is best used when the original wording is powerful, captures an important point, or when accuracy and precision are paramount. However, direct quotes should be used sparingly and only when it adds value to your argument.

For example, if a renowned scientist states, "Global warming is the greatest challenge of our time," it might be best to use a direct quote if it highlights the significance of the topic in your research.

Choosing Paraphrases:

A paraphrase involves restating the ideas or information from a research source using your own words. Paraphrasing lets you restate complex ideas or arguments in a more understandable manner while maintaining the accuracy of the original source. When paraphrasing, make sure you capture the key points of the source and correctly attribute the ideas to the original author.

For example, if a study concludes that a sedentary lifestyle increases the risk of chronic diseases, you could paraphrase it as "Living a physically inactive life heightens the chances of developing long-term health conditions."

Appropriately Using Direct Quotes and Paraphrases:

To use direct quotes and paraphrases properly, consider these best practices:

a. Avoid overusing direct quotes: It is important to maintain a balance between your original thoughts and the ideas of others. Overusing direct quotes can make your writing seem like a patchwork of someone else's work. Only use direct quotes when they enhance your argument or reinforce a specific point.

b. Introduce direct quotes: Before including a direct quote, provide context and introduce it. This helps the reader understand why you are including that specific quote and how it relates to your research.

c. Attribute sources: Always properly attribute direct quotes and paraphrases to their original sources. This can be done through in-text citations or footnotes, depending on the formatting style you are using (such as MLA, APA, or Chicago). Failing to attribute your sources can lead to accusations of plagiarism.

d. Maintain clarity and coherence: Ensure that the use of direct quotes and paraphrases contributes to the clarity and coherence of your argument. Avoid interrupting the flow of your writing with excessively long quotes. Use ellipses (…) to remove irrelevant sections from direct quotes while maintaining their original meaning.

e. Edit for seamless integration: When incorporating direct quotes and paraphrases, ensure they blend seamlessly with your writing style and voice. Use signal phrases to introduce quotations smoothly and adjust verb tenses and pronouns as necessary to maintain grammatical consistency.

Overall, using direct quotes and paraphrases correctly can significantly enhance the quality and credibility of your research. By integrating these best practices, you will create a well-balanced and informed research paper that accurately represents your understanding and the ideas of others.

USING RELIABLE SOURCES: UNDERSTANDING THE IMPORTANCE OF CREDIBLE & AUTHORITATIVE SOURCES FOR RESEARCH:

Research forms a cornerstone of information exploration and critical thinking. It helps us understand complex subjects, make informed decisions, and contribute to the growth of knowledge. However, not all sources of information are created equal. It is crucial to use reliable and authoritative sources to ensure the accuracy and credibility of our research. This article aims to highlight the significance of credible sources and provide guidance on evaluating their reliability.

Why Are Reliable Sources Important?

Using reliable sources is essential for several reasons:

Accuracy: Reliable sources undergo a rigorous vetting process and are based on factual information. They help make sure the content you are referring to is accurate, reducing the chances of relying on false or misleading information.

Credibility: Credible sources are authored by experts in their respective fields who have extensive knowledge and experience. Their work is respected and recognized within the academic and professional communities, lending credibility to the information they present.

Depth and Scope: Reliable sources provide in-depth information and cover a wide range of parts related to the research topic. They draw on extensive research, experiments, or peer-reviewed studies, ensuring a comprehensive understanding of the topic.

Objectivity: Credible sources strive for objectivity and present information without undue bias or personal opinions. They provide a balanced view that lets readers form their own judgments based on the presented evidence.

How to Evaluate the Reliability of Sources:

While understanding the importance of reliable sources is crucial, it is equally essential to develop the skills to evaluate their reliability. Here are key factors to consider when evaluating the credibility of information sources:

Author Credentials: Determine the author's qualifications, expertise, and affiliations. Look for degrees, research experience, and evidence of their authority in the topic.

Publication or Source Type: Consider the reputation of the publication or source. Peer-reviewed academic journals are highly regarded, as they undergo a rigorous review process by experts in the field. Government websites, reputable news outlets, and well-known research institutions are also reliable sources.

Objective vs. Biased Tone: Assess the source's tone for neutral and objective language. Biased language, sensationalism, or overly emotional appeals can show a lack of objectivity.

Citations and References: Look for citations and references that support the information provided. These should be recent, relevant, and from credible sources themselves.

Timeliness: Determine the currency of the information. Research evolves rapidly, so seek up-to-date sources, especially when dealing with scientific discoveries, technological advancements, or current events.

Cross-Referencing: Validate the information presented by cross-referencing it with multiple reliable sources. Consistency in the information across different sources increases its reliability.

Peer Review: For scholarly works, check if the article has undergone a peer-review process. This makes sure experts in the field have reviewed and validated the research before publication.

By using these evaluation techniques, researchers can confidently select reliable and authoritative sources to support their work, enhancing the overall credibility and validity of their research findings.

Utilizing reliable sources is critical for accurate and credible research. Understanding the importance of authoritative sources and assessing their reliability lets researchers make informed decisions and contribute to the advancement of knowledge. By honing our skills in source evaluation, we can navigate the vast sea of information and make sure our research is built on a solid foundation.

NAVIGATING THE CHALLENGES OF ONLINE RESEARCH TO EFFECTIVELY SEARCH FOR & CITE DIGITAL SOURCES:

In today's digital age, the internet has become a vast resource for information. However, with the abundance of readily available content online, it is essential to navigate the challenges and identify reliable sources. This section will discuss the unique challenges associated with finding accurate information online and provide strategies to effectively search for and cite digital sources.

The Challenge of Information Overload:

The internet is inundated with massive amounts of information, making it difficult to find credible sources. To overcome this challenge:

a. Start with reputable websites: Focus on reliable sources such as educational institutions, government websites, and established organizations.

b. Utilize advanced search techniques: Take advantage of search engine features like Boolean operators, quotation marks for exact phrase searches, and filtering options.

Evaluating Source Credibility:

Determining the credibility of online sources is crucial. Here's how to assess the reliability of digital information:

a. Examine the author's expertise: Look for credentials, qualifications, and relevant experience that establish the author's authority on the topic.

b. Verify the source's reputation: Check if the website or publisher has a solid track record and a reputation for providing accurate and unbiased information.

c. Assess currency and relevancy: Ensure that the information is up to date and relevant to your research topic.

Fact-Checking and Verification:

Misinformation and fake news are common online, so it is essential to fact-check and verify information. Consider the following:

a. Cross-reference information: Consult multiple reputable sources to verify the accuracy and consistency of the information you find.

b. Check for primary sources: Whenever possible, refer to primary sources such as research papers, official reports, or original documents to ensure accuracy.

c. Use fact-checking websites: Websites like Snopes or FactCheck.org can help identify misinformation and provide accurate information on various topics.

Effective Search Strategies:

To enhance your online research abilities, use these strategies for effective searching:

a. Use specific keywords: Instead of generic terms, use specific, relevant keywords that narrow down your search to obtain more targeted results.

b. Bonus: Enclose phrases in quotation marks: Quotation marks around phrases result in more precise searches by retrieving web pages containing the exact phrase.

c. Explore advanced search options: Take advantage of advanced search filters and tools offered by search engines to refine your results.

Citing Digital Sources:

Accurate citation of digital sources is essential for maintaining academic integrity. Consider these guidelines for citing digital sources:

a. Use proper citation styles: Consult specific citation style guides (APA, MLA, Chicago, etc.) to ensure consistent and accurate citation formatting.

b. Include relevant information: Provide the author's name, publication date, title, URL, and any other relevant details required by the citation style.

c. Use citation management tools: Use citation management tools like Zotero or EndNote to help organize and generate citations efficiently.

Online research presents unique challenges due to the vast amount of information, credibility concerns, and the need for accurate citation of digital sources. By using effective search strategies, critically evaluating sources, fact-checking, and properly citing digital sources, researchers can overcome these challenges and ensure the reliability and credibility of their work.

ENHANCING CREDIBILITY WITH PROPER CITATION FORMATTING FOR FORMATTING CITATIONS & REFERENCE LISTS ACCORDING TO DIFFERENT CITATION STYLES:

Enhancing Credibility with Proper Citation Formatting:

Exploring the impact of consistent and accurate citation formatting on the overall credibility of your work, including tips and guidelines for formatting citations and reference lists according to different citation styles.

Proper citation formatting is crucial for enhancing the credibility of your work. Accurate citations show you have conducted thorough research, respect intellectual property rights, and provide readers with the opportunity to verify your sources. This chapter explores the impact of consistent and accurate citation formatting on the overall credibility of your work, and provides tips and guidelines for formatting citations and reference lists according to different citation styles.

Establishing Credibility Through Accurate Citations:

Credible research relies on accurate citations. By citing sources correctly, you show you have used reliable and authoritative references to support your work. This enhances the credibility of your arguments and shows your commitment to academic integrity.

Consistency in Citation Formatting:

Consistency is key in citation formatting. By adhering to a specific citation style consistently throughout your work, you show attention to detail and professionalism. Consistency simplifies verifying your sources and makes sure your work is easily understood by others. Common citation styles include APA (American Psychological Association), MLA (Modern Language Association), and Chicago.

Tips and Guidelines for Formatting Citations:

a. APA style:

In-text citations: In APA style, include the author's last name and the year of publication within parentheses when citing a source directly (e.g., Smith, 2021). If you are citing a paraphrase or summary, you only need to include the author's last name and year.

Reference list: The reference list should include full bibliographic details for each cited source. Arrange the references in alphabetical order by the author's last name. Follow specific formatting guidelines for different types of sources (e.g., books, journal articles, websites).

b. MLA style:

In-text citations: MLA style typically uses the author's last name and page number in parentheses for in-text citations (e.g., Smith 14). If the author's name is mentioned in the sentence, only include the page number.

Works Cited page: MLA style requires a Works Cited page at the end of your work, listing all the sources you cited. Arrange the entries alphabetically by the author's last name. Follow specific formatting guidelines for different types of sources (e.g., books, articles, websites).

c. Chicago style:

Footnotes or endnotes: Chicago style uses footnotes or endnotes to cite sources. Each superscript number in the text corresponds to a numbered note containing the full citation information at the bottom of the page (footnotes) or at the end of the document (endnotes).

Bibliography: In addition to footnotes or endnotes, Chicago style requires a separate bibliography at the end of your work. This should include all the sources you cited, listed in alphabetical order by the author's last name.

Verifying Citation Formatting:

Before submitting your work, double-check your citations and reference list to ensure accuracy and consistency. Use citation generators or style guides specific to your chosen citation style to ensure proper formatting. Also, consider asking a peer or instructor to review your citations to catch any potential errors.

Consistent and accurate citation formatting significantly affects the credibility of your work. By properly citing your sources, you establish credibility, enhance the validity of your research, and respect intellectual property rights. Following the guidelines provided by different citation styles, such as APA, MLA, and Chicago, ensures proper citation formatting. By paying attention to these details, you elevate the professionalism and credibility of your work.

Chapter Summary:

Chapter 8 dives into the big deal of research citations. Here's why it matters:

Giving Credit: Citing sources is about thanking those who helped you and making sure you're not stealing ideas.

Making Your Argument Stronger: Citations back up your info and make folks trust you more.

Showing You Know Your Stuff: Proper citing is like saying, "I really know this topic."

Connecting Ideas: Citations build bridges between ideas, even in different fields.

Helping Future Research: Your work could pave the way for others.

Boosting Your Reputation: Playing by the rules builds respect.

But it's not just the why, it's the how. The chapter looks at four main citation styles: APA, MLA, Chicago, and IEEE. They've each got their rules, and you've got to nail them to make your work shine.

It also digs into in-text citations. That's how you show folks where you got your info in the actual text. Master this, and your writing will stand out.

Finally, the chapter goes into the details of direct quotes and paraphrases, and the importance of using reliable sources. You've got to get these right to give your writing a rock-solid foundation.

So, all in all, Chapter 8's not just a rulebook; it's a toolkit. It's like a roadmap to make your work top-notch. If you want to rock your academic writing, this chapter's got the goods. It's all about using the right sources and citing them the way they deserve.

In our Next Chapter...

Do you want to create a story that resonates with readers on an emotional level? Chapter 9 of this book is all about tapping into the power of emotional connections to craft stories that your readers won't forget.

This chapter explores the role of emotions in literature, showing how they can enhance the overall reading experience by helping readers explore and understand their own emotions and gain a deeper understanding of others. It also dives into the psychological factors behind different emotions, offering key insights into how writers can weave these feelings into their stories and create an emotional bond with readers.

From joy to sadness, fear to awe, this chapter shows how tapping into both positive and negative emotions is key to making characters your readers can relate to and root for. It also provides valuable tips on how to draw readers in and keep them hooked, such as using sensory details, crafting conflicts and dilemmas, and developing stories that show characters growing and learning.

This chapter isn't just a guide to fostering emotional connections; it's a deep dive into the human heart and mind. It offers valuable insights for writers looking to create stories with real emotional impact and for anyone interested in the power of storytelling.

So, if you want to take your writing to the next level, check out Chapter 9: Fostering Emotional Connections and explore how to create a story that leaves a lasting impression on your readers.

You'll be glad you did.

And don't forget that emotional connections are just as powerful in other forms of media too, like films and television shows. Knowing how to create strong emotions with storytelling can help you take your creative projects to the next level and craft stories that truly connect with people. So let this chapter be the start of your journey into the power of emotional connections.

CHAPTER NINE

FOSTERING EMOTIONAL CONNECTIONS: STRATEGIES FOR ELICITING AN EMOTIONAL RESPONSE FROM READERS TO CREATE A LASTING IMPACT

THE IMPORTANCE OF EMOTIONAL CONNECTIONS IN LITERATURE & HOW IT ENHANCES THE OVERALL READING EXPERIENCE.

THE IMPORTANCE of emotional connections in literature cannot be overstated. Through the power of storytelling, authors can create profound emotional experiences for their readers. By crafting relatable characters, depicting raw human emotions, and exploring universal themes, literature has the potential to elicit empathy and understanding from its audience.

One of the primary reasons emotional connections are essential in literature is that they draw readers deeper into the story. When readers can relate to the characters' struggles, joys, and sorrows, they become emotionally invested in their journey. This engagement not only makes sure the readers are more likely to continue reading but also fosters a sense of connection and identification with the narrative. As readers see themselves reflected in the characters' experiences, they are more likely to become emotionally and intellectually involved in the story.

Emotional connections in literature provide readers with an opportunity to explore and understand their own emotions. By exposing readers to a wide range of feelings, literature gives them a platform to process and make sense of their own emotional experiences. In this way, literature becomes a tool for emotional growth and self-reflection. When readers connect on an emotional level, they are more likely to remember and internalize the messages conveyed in the story, leading to a more profound reading experience.

In addition, emotional connections in literature can increase readers' empathy and understanding of others. By entering the minds and hearts of characters, readers gain insights into different perspectives, cultures, and experiences. Through this understanding, literature helps foster tolerance and empathy, as readers see the complexities of others' lives and emotions. By generating emotional connections, literature promotes compassion and helps with a more inclusive and diverse society.

Another significant advantage of emotional connections is the ability to create memorable and powerful moments in literature. When readers become emotionally invested in a story, they remember the characters, scenes, and messages long after they have read. These visceral and emotional experiences leave a lasting impact and contribute to a more meaningful reading experience. Such connections can inspire readers, spark conversations, and even influence personal growth.

The importance of emotional connections in literature cannot be overlooked. By fostering empathy, promoting self-reflection, increasing understanding of others, and providing memorable experiences, emotional connections enhance the overall reading experience. Literature has the power to transport readers to different worlds and, through emotional connections, invite them to appreciate the beauty and complexities of the human experience.

UNDERSTANDING READER EMOTIONS:

When readers engage with a text, they undergo a diverse range of emotions that can greatly affect their reading experience. Understanding these emotions and the psychological factors that influence them is crucial for writers to effectively connect with their audience and convey their message. In this section, we will explore the various emotions readers may experience and the underlying psychological factors that contribute to their emotional responses.

Positive Emotions:

Joy: Readers may feel joy when they encounter heartwarming or uplifting content that evokes happiness and delight.

Excitement: Engaging narratives, thrilling plot twists, and suspenseful storytelling can create excitement in readers.

Inspiration: Motivational messages or stories that depict individuals overcoming challenges can inspire readers and ignite their drive for personal growth.

Psychological factors: Positive emotions are often stimulated by the fulfillment of basic psychological needs, such as the need for competence, autonomy, and relatedness. When readers experience content that satisfies these needs, they are more likely to feel positive emotions.

Negative Emotions:

Sadness: Emotional narratives or stories of loss can evoke feelings of sadness and empathy in readers.

Fear: Suspense, horror, or stories involving danger and uncertainty can trigger fear and anxiety in readers.

Anger: Injustice, unfairness, or provocative themes can elicit anger or frustration in readers.

Psychological factors: Negative emotions can be linked to psychological factors like the need for control or the perception of injustice.

When readers encounter narratives that challenge their sense of control or highlight injustice, they might experience these negative emotions.

Empathy and Compassion:

Empathy: When readers connect with characters and their experiences, they can develop a sense of empathy, understanding, and sharing emotions.

Compassion: Depictions of characters facing adversity or suffering can evoke a reader's compassion and desire to provide support or help.

Psychological factors: Empathy and compassion are results of mirror neurons in the human brain, which enable individuals to emotionally resonate with others. When readers can relate to characters' emotions or experiences, they activate these mirror neurons and experience empathy or compassion.

Surprise:

Surprise: Unexpected plot twists, revelations, or unforeseen events can evoke surprise in readers, leading to heightened engagement and curiosity.

Psychological factors: Surprise arises from a discrepancy between readers' expectations and the actual content. When readers receive information that deviates from their expected narrative direction, it triggers surprise.

Awe:

Awe: Extraordinary or breathtaking descriptions, unique perspectives, or immense beauty can inspire awe in readers, giving them a sense of wonder and reverence.

Psychological factors: Awe is often experienced when individuals encounter something larger than themselves or when they feel an expansion of their mental boundaries. When texts encompass grand ideas or provide a sense of transcendence, readers can experience awe.

Understanding the range of emotions readers may experience while reading, as well as the psychological factors that contribute to these emotional responses, lets writers create content that resonates deeply with their audience. By skillfully crafting narratives that evoke specific emotions, writers can establish a stronger connection, convey their messages effectively, and leave a lasting impact on their readers.

CRAFTING RELATABLE CHARACTERS THAT READERS CAN EMOTIONALLY CONNECT WITH, SUCH AS GIVING THEM RELATABLE FLAWS, DESIRES, & FEARS.

Crafting relatable characters is essential for creating a strong emotional connection between readers and the story. When readers can empathize with a character's flaws, desires, and fears, they become invested in their journey. Here are effective strategies for developing characters that readers can emotionally connect with:

Flaws: Give characters relatable flaws that make them human and flawed. Flaws create empathy because readers see parts of themselves in the characters. Whether it's being overly critical, impulsive, or indecisive, flaws make characters relatable, and relatability creates emotional connections.

Desires: Characters with relatable desires that readers can identify with are more engaging. Readers want to see characters striving for something they can understand and resonate with. These desires could be universal, such as love, acceptance, success, or more specific, like finding a sense of belonging or reconnecting with a lost loved one.

Fears: Explore the fears and anxieties of your characters to evoke emotions from readers. Fear is a powerful motivator and something everyone can relate to. Whether it's the fear of failure, rejection, or loss, these fears make characters vulnerable and human, letting readers connect with their struggles.

Backstory: Provide a well-developed backstory that explains why characters have the flaws, desires, and fears they have. Understanding their past experiences enables readers to understand and empathize with their actions, making them more emotionally invested in their growth and journey.

Conflict: Create conflicts that challenge the characters emotionally. By placing characters in situations that force them to confront their flaws, desires, and fears, readers can see their growth and transformation. This growth helps readers form strong emotional connections by rooting for characters to overcome their internal struggles.

Relatable dialogues: Use realistic dialogue that captures the way people truly speak and think. Authentic conversations make characters feel relatable, letting readers connect with their thoughts and emotions. Avoid clichés and overly formal language, instead, focus on creating dialogues that reflect the character's personality and experiences.

Vulnerability: Allow characters to be vulnerable and show their emotions. Readers connect with characters open about their fears and insecurities, as it makes them more authentic and relatable. Emotional vulnerability helps readers connect on a deeper level, evoking empathy and understanding.

Growth and development: Characters should evolve throughout the story, learning from their experiences and overcoming their flaws or fears. Readers find satisfaction in seeing characters grow and change, as it reflects the personal growth they aspire to achieve in their own lives.

Relatable characters come from a place of authenticity and emotional truth. Developing characters with relatable flaws, desires, and fears lets readers see themselves in those characters, creating a strong emotional bond that keeps them invested throughout the story.

EMPLOYING VIVID SENSORY DESCRIPTIONS TO EVOKE EMOTIONAL RESPONSES FROM READERS, ALLOWING THEM TO FEEL MORE DEEPLY CONNECTED TO THE NARRATIVE:

Using descriptive language that appeals to the senses is a powerful tool in crafting a narrative that resonates deeply with readers. By using vivid sensory descriptions, a writer can evoke emotional responses and create a strong connection between the reader and the story being conveyed.

One way descriptive language connects with readers is through engaging their senses. When a writer describes a scene in a way that triggers the reader's senses, it immediately pulls them into the narrative. It lets readers envision the scene in their minds, creating a more immersive reading experience.

For example, imagine a writer describing a beautiful sunset with vivid sensory details. They might describe the warm hues of red, orange, and purple lining the sky, the gentle breeze carrying the scent of blooming flowers, and the sound of birds chirping and leaves rustling. By painting such a vivid picture with words, the writer is not only appealing to the reader's imagination but also tapping into their emotive senses.

By engaging the senses, readers are more likely to feel connected to the narrative on an emotional level. They may experience a sense of awe or wonder at the beauty of the sunset, or a feeling of peace and tranquility as they imagine the gentle breeze and soothing sounds. These emotional responses are crucial in creating a deeper connection between the reader and the story.

Additionally, descriptive language that appeals to the senses can elicit emotional responses unique to each reader. As each person may have different sensory experiences in the real world, the individualized responses to descriptive language can enhance the reader's personal connection to the narrative. One reader may resonate more with the visual imagery, while another may be deeply moved by the description of sounds or scents. This variability lets readers relate to the narrative in their own way, forming a more personal and meaningful connection.

Sensory descriptions can also intensify the emotional impact of a narrative by creating a contrast between different senses. For example, a writer might describe a character's experience of walking barefoot on a sandy beach, feeling the soft and grainy texture under their feet while hearing the crashing waves and tasting the salty ocean air. This contrast between the senses can evoke a range of emotions, such as a sense of freedom, joy, or even nostalgia.

Utilizing descriptive language that appeals to the senses is a powerful technique to evoke emotional responses and establish a profound connection between readers and narratives. By engaging the senses, readers can visualize, hear, smell, taste, and feel the world being portrayed, enhancing their emotional involvement and personal connection to the story. Sensory descriptions create an immersive experience that lets readers feel more deeply connected to the narrative, fostering a lasting impact on their hearts and minds.

CREATING COMPELLING CONFLICTS AND DILEMMAS THAT RESONATE WITH READERS ON AN EMOTIONAL LEVEL, ENCOURAGING THEM TO BECOME EMOTIONALLY INVESTED IN THE OUTCOME.

Creating compelling conflicts and dilemmas is vital to engaging readers on an emotional level and encouraging them to become emotionally invested in the outcome of a story. Such conflicts and dilemmas drive the plot, generate tension, and let readers connect with the characters and their struggles. Here are five key elements to consider when developing conflicts and dilemmas that resonate with readers:

Understand your target audience: To create conflicts that resonate, it's crucial to understand your target audience's interests, values, and desires. What kinds of conflicts would they find relatable and emotionally engaging? Knowing your readers will help you craft conflicts that will captivate them.

Create high stakes: The conflicts and dilemmas must have significant consequences for the characters involved. These consequences can be physical, emotional, or psychological. When the stakes are high, readers feel more invested as they fear the outcome could significantly affect the characters they care about.

Make it personal for your characters: A conflict that affects the protagonist's deeply held beliefs, values, or relationships is more likely to evoke an emotional response from readers. By embedding the conflict into the characters' core identity, you create a situation that readers can emotionally connect with.

Show conflicting goals and desires: Conflicts arise when characters have opposing goals or desires. This creates tension as readers become invested in discovering how the conflict will be resolved. By showing the motivations and desires of both sides, readers can weigh the choices, sympathize with the characters, and become emotionally involved in the outcome.

Challenge readers' own beliefs and values: One effective way to engage readers emotionally is to create conflicts and dilemmas that challenge their own beliefs, values, or biases. When readers are forced to confront their own principles through the characters' struggles, they become emotionally invested in seeing how the conflict unfolds and seeking a resolution.

By combining these elements, you can create conflicts and dilemmas that resonate deeply with readers, drawing them into your story and encouraging them to emotionally invest in its outcome. Through these emotional connections, readers are more likely to feel a sense of satisfaction or catharsis when the conflicts are resolved, leading to a more fulfilling reading experience.

ENGAGING IN STORYTELLING TECHNIQUES THAT CAN INTENSIFY EMOTIONAL RESPONSES & ENSURE A LASTING IMPACT ON READERS:

Storytelling is an art form that captures the imagination and emotions of readers. One of the key aspects of a captivating story lies in the effective use of various techniques that intensify emotional responses and ensure a lasting impact. Three such techniques that enrich storytelling are foreshadowing, suspense, and dramatic tension.

Foreshadowing is a powerful tool that authors use to hint at future events, creating anticipation and curiosity in readers. By sprinkling subtle clues throughout the narrative, authors not only engage readers but also prepare them for what lies ahead. Foreshadowing builds suspense, making readers eager to uncover the mysteries it unveils. A classic example of foreshadowing is found in J.K. Rowling's "Harry Potter" series. In the first book, "Harry Potter and the Philosopher's Stone," hints about the villainous character of Professor Quirrell are dropped throughout the story, preparing readers for the eventual revelation of his true nature.

Suspense is another storytelling technique that keeps readers on the edge of their seats. It involves creating a sense of anticipation and anxiety regarding events yet to unfold. Suspense is often achieved through a combination of unanswered questions, unexpected twists, and upcoming dangers. Agatha Christie, the queen of suspense, expertly used this technique in her murder mysteries, leaving readers guessing until the very end. By skillfully manipulating information and building tension, suspense hooks readers and ensures they remain fully engaged with the story.

Dramatic tension is a technique that arises from conflicts, dilemmas, and clashes between characters or circumstances. It heightens emotional responses by capturing readers' attention and fostering a powerful emotional connection. Dramatic tension can be created through contrasting characters, conflicting motives, or internal struggles faced by protagonists. A prime example is found in the novel "To Kill a Mockingbird" by Harper Lee, where the tension between Scout Finch's innocence and the racial prejudices of her society evokes strong emotional responses from readers.

In combination, these storytelling techniques work synergistically to evoke powerful emotional responses and ensure a lasting impact on readers. When used effectively, foreshadowing sets the stage, suspense keeps the readers intrigued, and dramatic tension draws them into the story's conflicts. The skillful use of these techniques enables authors to develop an emotional connection between the readers and the narrative, resulting in a memorable reading experience.

Storytelling techniques such as foreshadowing, suspense, and dramatic tension are vital in crafting a compelling narrative. By deploying these techniques effectively, authors can intensify emotional responses, captivate readers, and leave a lasting impact. Whether it is through subtly hinting at future events, keeping readers in suspense, or creating intense conflicts, these techniques help to make sure a story resonates deeply with its audience.

Encouraging empathy and perspective-taking enabling the reader to forge emotional connections with characters and their experiences.

It has become increasingly important to encourage empathy and perspective-taking among individuals. Empathy, the ability to understand and share the feelings of others, is a crucial skill that promotes understanding, cooperation, and compassion. One powerful tool that can foster empathy is the use of narratives.

Narratives, whether in the form of books, movies, or even personal stories, have a great potential to create emotional connections between readers and characters. By presenting diverse perspectives and tackling challenging themes, narratives let readers step into the shoes of different characters and witness their experiences firsthand. This immersive experience enables readers to develop a deeper understanding of others, breaking down barriers and defying stereotypes.

When readers encounter characters from diverse backgrounds or find themselves in unfamiliar situations through narratives, they are prompted to reflect on their own preconceived notions and biases. They are challenged to question their assumptions and consider alternative viewpoints. This process broadens their perspective by exposing them to different cultures, beliefs, and life experiences.

By exploring diverse perspectives, narratives can also tackle difficult topics such as discrimination, inequality, and social injustice. Through these stories, readers are given the opportunity to engage with and emotionally connect to characters facing adversity or injustice. This emotional connection not only fosters empathy but also motivates readers to act, to stand against injustices they may have been unaware of or indifferent to.

Narratives let readers witness the growth and development of characters as they navigate various challenges. This journey not only resonates with readers on a personal level but also lets them empathize with the struggles and triumphs of the characters. It reinforces the idea that everyone faces their own battles and encourages readers to be more supportive and understanding toward others.

To encourage empathy and perspective-taking, it is vital to promote diverse narratives across various platforms. In schools, educators can include literature and films from different cultures, highlighting the experiences of marginalized groups. Through book clubs or discussion groups, readers can engage in thoughtful conversations, sharing their perspectives and learning from others.

Additionally, media outlets play a significant role in promoting empathy through narratives. By providing platforms for diverse voices to be heard and sharing stories that challenge existing biases, media can inspire viewers or readers to step out of their comfort zones and broaden their understanding of the world.

Narratives have the power to encourage empathy and perspective-taking by presenting diverse perspectives and addressing challenging themes. They let readers forge emotional connections with characters and their experiences, breaking down barriers, and promoting understanding. By recognizing and using the power of storytelling, we can foster a more empathetic and compassionate society.

Chapter Summary:

Creating emotional connections with readers is the goal of Chapter 10, which examines how they can help enhance the overall reading experience. Emotional connections give readers a chance to see themselves in the characters and strive for personal growth and build empathy and understanding of others. They also make literature more meaningful by leaving lasting impressions on readers.

To create these connections, writers should understand the different emotions readers may feel, including joy, excitement, inspiration, sadness, fear, anger, empathy, compassion, surprise and awe. Understanding the psychological factors behind these feelings is essential to crafting stories that resonate with readers.

This chapter provides insight into how writers can make characters their readers care about: by giving them flaws and desires, making them face their fears, having a backstory that explains why they are the way they are, creating conflicts and dilemmas, speaking like real people, showing emotions openly and allowing characters to change. Additionally, readers can be drawn in with sensory details, storytelling tricks, foreshadowing and suspense.

By mastering these techniques and nailing the emotional connections, writers can create stories that hit people right in the heart. Readers will feel for the characters, believe in the world created and be drawn into the struggles presented. This makes readers remember these stories long after they've finished them. Chapter 10 is a deep dive into understanding how to get readers emotionally invested in literature and make reading meaningful.

In our Next Chapter...

Discover the secret to compelling writing in Chapter 11: a goldmine of expert tips and strategies to elevate your prose and capture your audience's attention. Learn how to simplify complex ideas, introduce clarity in your sentences, and cut through the jargon. Discover how to tailor your writing to your readers, ensuring your message resounds deeply with them.

But that's not all! Chapter 11 also dives into how to make your writing uniquely yours. Discover how to infuse your personality into every word and every sentence, making your narrative distinctive and engaging. Explore different writing styles, gather feedback, and don't fear change - adapt to make it perfect.

If you're an aspiring writer looking to enhance your craft, or simply craving to make your work more authentic and relatable, Chapter 11 is your guide. Expect tips on creating vivid imagery that transports readers into your story, crafting memorable characters, and managing pace and tension to keep your readers hooked.

Remember, great writing comes from effective editing. Chapter 11 prepares you to become your own best critic, teaching you how to refine structure, eliminate repetition, and polish your work to perfection.

So, are you ready to make your words impactful, relatable, and unforgettably yours? Dive into Chapter 11 and transform your writing into a compelling and engaging narrative. Let's make your words hit home!

CHAPTER TEN

KEEPING READERS ENGAGED: TECHNIQUES FOR MAINTAINING READER INTEREST THROUGHOUT THE BOOK, INCLUDING PACING, STORYTELLING, & VARYING WRITING STYLES

THE IMPORTANCE OF ENGAGING READERS FROM THE VERY BEGINNING: EXPLORING EFFECTIVE OPENINGS THAT GRAB READERS' ATTENTION & MOTIVATE THEM TO CONTINUE READING:

THE IMPORTANCE of engaging readers from the beginning cannot be overstated. In a world flooded with information and distractions, capturing readers' attention from the start is crucial. The opening lines of a piece must serve as the gateway to a world of imagination, inspiring readers to continue reading and discover the wonders that await them.

An effective opening is like a magnetic force pulling readers in. It must intrigue, inspire, and ignite curiosity within the readers' minds. Whether it is a captivating anecdote, a thought-provoking question, or a powerful statement, the opening sets the tone for the entire piece. It is the first impression that can make or break the readers' interest.

By creating an opening that grabs readers' attention, writers establish a strong connection from the outset. This connection fosters an emotional investment in the readers, making them eager to explore the rest of the piece. Without this initial engagement, readers are more likely to abandon the piece and move on to something else.

A compelling opening motivates readers to seek knowledge, explore new perspectives, or indulge in the writer's world. It creates a sense of anticipation and compels readers to discover what lies ahead. It triggers their curiosity and ignites a desire to unravel the story or argument presented in the writing.

Great writers understand the power of a well-crafted opening, and they use various techniques to captivate their audience. Some may use vivid imagery to paint a mental picture, others may use an unexpected twist to subvert readers' expectations. The key is to strike a chord with the readers and make them realize that what they are about to read is different, important, and engaging.

In the digital age, where attention spans are shorter than ever, the importance of engaging readers from the beginning becomes even more vital. With endless distractions at their fingertips, readers need a compelling reason to invest their time and attention. An enticing opening is the perfect catalyst for this investment.

A powerful and attention-grabbing opening is essential to motivate readers to continue reading. It sparks enthusiasm, builds connections, and fuels curiosity. By engaging readers from the beginning, writers can make sure their message, story, or argument is not only heard but also fully embraced by their audience. So next time you embark on a writing journey, remember the significance of an effective opening and seize the opportunity to grab your readers' attention from the start.

USING PACING TECHNIQUES TO MAINTAIN READER INTEREST TO CREATE TENSION, SUSPENSE, OR EMOTIONAL IMPACT:

Pacing is a crucial element in writing that can greatly affect a reader's engagement and overall experience with a narrative. By strategically using pacing techniques, writers can effectively create tension, suspense, and emotional impact within their stories. This chapter aims to explore how slowing down or speeding up the narrative can achieve these effects.

Slowing down the narrative:

Slowing down the pace of the story can create tension and heighten suspense. By providing detailed descriptions, giving deeper insight into characters' thoughts and emotions, or prolonging a crucial moment, writers can build anticipation and engage readers at a deeper level.

a. Descriptive details: Elaborating on the environment, character appearances, or sensory details can slow down the pace. This technique immerses the reader in the story, helping them visualize the scene vividly. The increased focus on intricate details can create an atmospheric effect, adding to the overall tension.

b. Internal monologues: Introspection and reflection can be powerful tools for slowing down the narrative. When characters delve into their thoughts or emotions, readers gain a deeper understanding of their motivations and conflicts. This technique adds layers to the story and intensifies emotional impact, especially during critical moments.

c. Stretching suspenseful events: By prolonging a suspenseful event, writers keep readers on the edge of their seats. Building up to a climax slowly and deliberately can generate an increased sense of anticipation. It allows for tension to rise steadily, making the eventual resolution even more satisfying.

Speeding up the narrative:

Speeding up the pace of the story is equally important in maintaining reader interest. Quickening the tempo can create excitement, grab attention, and propel the storyline forward. However, it requires a careful balance to avoid overwhelming readers or sacrificing important details.

a. Shorter sentences and paragraphs: Using concise sentences and paragraphs can create a sense of urgency and increase the speed of the narrative. This technique is particularly effective during action sequences or intense moments, as it mimics the swift nature of events.

b. Dialogue and quick exchanges: Conversations infused with energy and tension help propel the story forward. Quick, snappy dialogue exchanges build momentum and keep readers engaged. This technique also provides an opportunity for character development and conflict resolution.

c. Swift transitions: By seamlessly transitioning between scenes or significant events, writers can maintain a fast-paced narrative. Avoiding long explanations or unnecessary details lets the story flow smoothly, capturing readers' attention and sustaining their interest.

Pacing is a powerful tool to maintain reader interest and evoke specific emotions. By alternating between slowing down and speeding up the narrative, writers can effectively create tension, suspense, or emotional impact. Careful consideration of these pacing techniques can enhance a story, making it a compelling and engaging experience for readers.

THE POWER OF STORYTELLING TO CAPTIVATE READERS & KEEP THEM INVESTED IN THE NARRATIVE:

Storytelling is an art, a mesmerizing force with the ability to transport us to different worlds, invoke emotions, and leave a lasting impact on our minds. It is the fundamental essence of human communication, dating back to ancient times when tales were shared around campfires. In this section, we will explore the integral elements of effective story-telling, including character development, plot twists, and vivid descriptions, to understand how they captivate readers and keep them invested in the narrative.

Character Development:

Characters are the lifeblood of any story, as readers crave relatable and compelling protagonists. Effective character development involves creating multi-dimensional individuals with depth, flaws, and desires.

Through well-crafted personalities, readers form emotional connections, investing in their journeys and eagerly following their growth throughout the narrative.

Plot Twists:

Plot twists are the unexpected turns in a story that leave readers shocked, awestruck, and hungry for more. These surprises disrupt predictable patterns and challenge readers' assumptions, injecting a sense of excitement and anticipation. Masterful plot twists are not only unexpected but also organic, seamlessly woven into the narrative arc, giving readers a thrilling experience while keeping them engaged.

Vivid Descriptions:

A story comes alive when we can vividly imagine the sights, sounds, and emotions present within it. Vivid descriptions serve as the window to the world the author has created for the readers. Through carefully crafted visuals, authors evoke sensory experiences, transporting readers into the heart of the story. Enhanced descriptions stimulate the reader's imagination, letting them visualize the scenery, feel the emotions, and experience a deeper connection to the narrative.

Pacing and Tension:

A well-paced story is crucial for maintaining readers' engagement. Balancing moments of intense action with periods of reflection or character development builds tension, creating a rollercoaster of emotions that holds readers captive. By carefully manipulating the timing of events, authors generate anticipation and keep readers invested, ensuring they are eager to turn every page.

Authenticity and Meaning:

An effective story transcends its superficial parts and resonates on a deeper level. By reflecting real human experiences, emotions, and challenges, storytelling taps into universal truths that connect us all. By injecting authenticity and meaning into the narrative, authors let readers relate and find personal connections in the story, making it an unforgettable experience.

Effective storytelling is a potent tool that can capture readers' hearts and minds, taking them on unforgettable journeys filled with excitement, empathy, and introspection. Through elements like well-developed characters, plot twists, vivid descriptions, and authentic narratives, authors create a powerful bond between their words and the readers. As we continue to explore the magic of storytelling, it becomes apparent that its power lies in its ability to captivate, inspire, and leave an indelible mark on our lives.

VARYING WRITING STYLES FOR ADDED ENGAGEMENT TO INTRIGUE READERS & PROVIDE A MORE DYNAMIC READING EXPERIENCE:

Writing is an art form that continues to evolve, with writers constantly seeking innovative ways to captivate their audience. One effective technique for engaging readers is incorporating varying writing styles into their work. By weaving in elements such as dialogue, flashbacks, and first-person narration, writers can provide a more dynamic reading experience and intrigue their audience in unexpected ways.

One way to pique a reader's interest is through dialogue. Dialogue allows for a direct interaction between characters, bringing them to life and adding depth to the narrative. Through dialogue, readers can gain insights into characters' personalities, motivations, and conflicts. This not only enhances the storytelling but also creates a connection between readers and the characters, drawing them further into the story.

Another technique that can engage readers is the use of flashbacks. Flashbacks offer glimpses into a character's past, letting readers understand their backstory and motivations. By introducing these moments of remembrance, writers can create suspense, reveal secrets, or build emotional connections. Flashbacks add layers to the narrative, making it more compelling and nuanced.

Incorporating first-person narration is yet another writing style that can enhance reader engagement. By presenting the story from the perspective of a single character, writers can provide a more intimate and immersive experience. This narrative style lets readers see the world through the protagonist's eyes, experiencing their emotions, thoughts, and desires firsthand. This direct connection with the main character lets readers form a strong bond and become emotionally invested in the story.

Combining these various writing styles creates a multi-dimensional reading experience, keeping readers captivated throughout the narrative. It breaks the monotony of a single tone or perspective, adding variety and excitement. By skillfully integrating dialogue, flashbacks, and first-person narration, writers can create a story not only engaging but also thought-provoking and memorable.

Different writing styles can convey information and evoke emotions in unique ways. Dialogue, for example, allows for natural and immediate exchanges, which can effectively reveal conflicts between characters or highlight key plot points. On the other hand, flashbacks offer a more reflective and introspective tone, providing opportunities for character development and emotional resonance. First-person narration, with its personal and subjective nature, enables readers to intimately connect with the protagonist's journey, sharing their joys, fears, and triumphs.

Ultimately, the benefits of incorporating varying writing styles lie in their ability to intrigue readers, provide a more dynamic reading experience, and deeply involve them in the story. By masterfully blending dialogue, flashbacks, and first-person narration, writers can create a narrative that keeps readers on the edge of their seats, eagerly turning the pages to uncover what lies beneath the surface. So, next time you embark on a writing journey, consider exploring different writing styles to inspire, engage, and leave a lasting impact on your readers.

THE ROLE OF CONFLICTS & OBSTACLES THAT READERS ARE EAGER TO SEE RESOLVED, MAINTAINING THEIR ENGAGEMENT:

Conflicts and obstacles play a vital role in any book as they create tension, keep readers engaged, and drive the story forward. When conflicts and obstacles are introduced and developed effectively, they can create a sense of anticipation and eagerness among readers to see them resolved. This section delves into how conflicts and obstacles shape a story and maintain reader engagement.

First, conflicts and obstacles create stakes. When characters face challenges or conflicts, it adds depth to their journey and gives readers a reason to invest in their outcome. These conflicts can vary from external ones, such as a physical threat or a major problem to solve, to internal conflicts like self-doubt or moral dilemmas. By presenting these obstacles, authors portray the consequences characters may face if they fail or succeed, which generates a sense of anticipation and curiosity among readers.

Additionally, conflicts and obstacles introduce unpredictability. When a story becomes predictable, readers may lose interest. By introducing conflicts and obstacles, authors add elements of surprise and uncertainty, keeping readers on the edge of their seats. Unpredictability creates tension and makes sure readers will continue turning the pages to discover how the characters overcome the challenges they face.

Conflicts and obstacles provide opportunities for character development. As characters navigate through difficulties, they evolve and grow, adding depth and complexity to their personalities. Seeing their struggle and eventual growth lets readers form emotional connections with the characters. Readers become emotionally invested in their journey and are eager to see them overcome the obstacles in their path.

Conflicts and obstacles allow for pacing and plot advancement. Without conflicts, stories can become stagnant and lose momentum. By strategically placing obstacles throughout the book, authors can maintain a steady pace and a continuous flow of action. Engaging conflicts and obstacles keep readers engrossed, ensuring they remain fully committed to the story until the resolution.

Last, conflicts and obstacles create tension and release. As readers expect the resolution of a conflict or obstacle, tension builds up. This tension often serves as an incentive for readers to continue reading. When the conflict is ultimately resolved, it provides a sense of release or satisfaction, rewarding readers for their investment in the story.

Conflicts and obstacles are essential in creating engaging narratives. By introducing and developing conflicts and obstacles, authors create stakes, add unpredictability, drive character development, maintain pacing, and create tension and release. Through these elements, readers are kept eager to see how the conflicts and obstacles are resolved, maintaining their engagement and ensuring they stay connected to the story until its conclusion.

BUILDING TENSION AND SUSPENSE TO KEEP READERS HOOKED & EAGER TO DISCOVER WHAT HAPPENS NEXT:

Building tension and suspense is a vital element in keeping readers engaged and eager to uncover what happens next in a story. Using various techniques such as foreshadowing, cliffhangers, and unexpected plot twists, writers can effectively hook their audience and create a captivating reading experience. Let's delve into each technique and explore how they contribute to building tension and suspense.

Foreshadowing: Foreshadowing is a technique that hints at future events or outcomes in a subtle way. By planting these hints throughout the narrative, writers create anticipation and a sense of foreboding. Foreshadowing can take many forms, including subtle clues, symbolic imagery, or even character dialogue. When readers notice these hints, they become engrossed in predicting and speculating about what will happen later on.

Cliffhangers: Cliffhangers occur at the end of a section or chapter, leaving readers hanging on the edge of their seat and desperate to discover what happens next. By abruptly interrupting a scene just when it reaches a crucial point or revealing a shocking revelation right before cutting off, writers effectively heighten tension. The unresolved nature of a cliffhanger compels readers to continue reading, eager to see the resolution unfold.

Unexpected plot twists: Introducing unexpected plot twists can completely shift the direction of a story, surprising readers and injecting a new dose of tension. These twists can come in various forms, such as a sudden betrayal, a shocking revelation, or a major turning point. By breaking the reader's expectations and overturning established assumptions, unexpected plot twists keep readers on their toes and maintain a constant state of suspense.

Timing: Timing is crucial when building and sustaining tension. It's essential to balance the pace of the story, letting tension rise steadily but providing occasional moments of relief. Too much tension with no release can exhaust readers, while too little tension can cause them to lose interest. Skillful pacing makes sure readers are continually engaged and eager to discover what unfolds next.

Character development: Crafting well-rounded and relatable characters can also contribute to building tension and suspense. When readers become invested in the characters' journeys, their emotional involvement increases. Writers can use this emotional connection to manipulate tension by putting the characters in perilous situations or creating internal conflicts that resonate with readers.

Conflict and stakes: Introducing conflicts and raising the stakes heightens tension by presenting obstacles that the characters must overcome. Whether it's a life-or-death situation, a high-stakes competition, or a tense confrontation between characters, escalating conflicts add to the sense of suspense. By making the outcome uncertain or dire, writers make sure readers are continually invested in the story.

By skillfully using techniques like foreshadowing, cliffhangers, unexpected plot twists, well-timed pacing, compelling characters, and heightened conflicts, writers can effectively build and sustain tension and suspense in their narratives. This keeps the readers hooked, activating their curiosity and desire to discover what happens next. Ultimately, a well-crafted story that keeps readers engaged with its tension and suspense is more likely to captivate and leave a lasting impact.

BALANCING ACTION AND QUIETER MOMENTS THAT KEEP READERS ENGAGED BY OFFERING A VARIETY OF EXPERIENCES & EMOTIONS.

To create a well-rounded and captivating narrative, it's crucial to balance action-packed scenes and quieter, introspective moments. These two elements work in tandem, offering readers a variety of experiences and emotions that keep them engaged throughout the story.

Action-packed scenes are essential for injecting excitement, tension, and a sense of urgency into the narrative. These moments often involve high stakes, intense conflicts, and physical challenges, propelling the story forward at a brisk pace. Whether it's an adrenaline-fueled battle sequence, a thrilling chase, or a heart-pounding escape, these scenes grab readers' attention and make them feel as if they are right in the action.

However, it is equally important to incorporate quieter, introspective moments between the action. These moments let readers delve deeper into the characters' thoughts, emotions, and motivations. Through introspection, readers gain a more profound understanding of the characters' internal struggles, fears, and desires. This helps in developing complex and relatable characters, fostering empathy and creating a stronger emotional connection between the readers and the story.

Introspective moments also serve as a narrative tool for reflection and insight. They provide an opportunity for characters to assess their situations, make important decisions, or ponder over past events. These quieter moments let readers catch their breath, digest information, and contemplate the implications of the action-packed scenes they have experienced.

By incorporating both action-packed scenes and quieter, introspective moments, the narrative gains a natural ebb and flow, mirroring the dynamics of real life. This balance makes sure readers remain engaged and interested throughout the story, as they are constantly entertained by the thrill of action and provided with opportunities to reflect and connect with characters on a deeper level.

The alternation between action and introspection allows the narrative to build tension more effectively. Intense action scenes can serve as climactic moments, followed by quieter intervals that heighten the anticipation, creating a rhythm that drives the story forward. This pacing technique keeps readers hooked, eager to know what will happen next, while also providing meaningful pauses for them to process and appreciate the story's emotional depth.

Balancing action-packed scenes and quieter, introspective moments is essential in crafting a well-paced narrative that keeps readers engaged. By providing a variety of experiences and emotions, this balance captivates readers, ensuring they are constantly entertained, emotionally invested, and eagerly turning the pages. So, whether injecting thrilling action or providing moments of introspection, incorporating both elements is key to creating a narrative that resonates with readers long after they finish the story.

Chapter Summary:

Engaging Readers from the Start: Captivating readers from the beginning is crucial. Effective openings with anecdotes, questions, or statements set the tone and spark curiosity. In today's information-rich digital era, a compelling start is even more vital to establish an emotional connection with readers.

Mastering Pacing Techniques: Pacing controls the rhythm and speed of a story. Slowing down through detailed descriptions and internal monologues builds tension, while speeding up with quick dialogue and swift transitions creates excitement. Skillful pacing ensures a balanced blend of tension, suspense, and emotional impact, enhancing reader engagement.

Unleashing the Power of Storytelling: Storytelling, an ancient art, captivates readers through character development, plot twists, vivid descriptions, and well-crafted pacing. Creating multi-dimensional characters, unexpected yet organic plot twists, and evocative descriptions immerses readers in the story.

Authenticity and meaning resonate deeply, reflecting universal truths and human connections. These three elements highlight the significance of connecting with readers from the outset, maintaining their interest with effective pacing, and harnessing the profound power of storytelling.

Mastering these techniques elevates writing, leaving readers with a memorable and meaningful experience. Writing a gripping story goes beyond mere words on paper; it requires creating a vibrant world that keeps readers enthralled.

The magic lies in blending elements to provide readers with a thrilling and thought-provoking journey. So, how can you achieve that? Start by utilizing dialogue to reveal characters' personalities and forge connections. Sprinkle in flashbacks to add suspense and depth to the narrative. Experiment with first-person narration to establish a strong bond between readers and characters, evoking empathy and interest. Embrace conflicts and obstacles as catalysts for progress and character development. These elements inject excitement, unpredictability, and growth, ensuring the story remains captivating.

Remember to balance tension and suspense, employing techniques like cliffhangers and unexpected plot twists, while maintaining a well-paced narrative to sustain reader engagement. Strike a harmonious equilibrium between action-packed sequences and quieter moments of introspection. Action scenes infuse excitement and tension, while reflective interludes allow readers to delve into characters' thoughts and emotions.

This rhythmic interplay maintains reader interest and emotional connection. Ultimately, the goal is to provide readers with a multi-dimensional experience. By exploring diverse writing styles and techniques, you can craft a story that is engaging, memorable, and impactful.

Whether you are an experienced writer or just starting out, embrace experimentation to discover what works best for your narrative. The journey will be rewarding!

In our Next Chapter...

Unlock the secrets to captivating prose in Chapter 11: Perfecting Your Writing Style: Tips for Enhancing Your Prose, Refining Your Voice, & Making Your Writing More CompellingDo you yearn to refine your prose and develop a unique writing voice that captures readers' imaginations? Look no further than Chapter 11 of our writing guide, which delves into the mastery of style and the craft of compelling storytelling.

In this valuable chapter, you'll learn:

- The power of clarity - Tips for enhancing accessibility through clear language and simplified sentence structures
- Finding your voice - Strategies to develop an authentic style that resonates with readers
- Vivid imagery - Harness figurative language and sensory details to paint an immersive world
- Storytelling mastery - Plot, character, and tension techniques to construct gripping narratives
- Rhythm and flow - Sentence pacing and dialogue to grab attention and build engagement
- Editing like a pro - Revise and refine your work to elevate quality and maximize impact
- The art of experimentation - How to evolve your writing through practice, feedback, and pushing boundaries

Follow the guidance in Chapter 11 to transform your prose. Say goodbye to lackluster writing and embrace your potential as a captivating storyteller. The journey toward stylistic mastery starts here!

∿

PERFECTING YOUR WRITING STYLE: TIPS FOR ENHANCING YOUR PROSE, REFINING YOUR VOICE, & MAKING YOUR WRITING MORE COMPELLING

UNDERSTANDING THE IMPORTANCE OF CLARITY AND SIMPLICITY IN WRITING TO MAKE YOUR WRITING MORE ACCESSIBLE & ENGAGING.

IN THE REALM of effective writing, clarity and simplicity are paramount. By eliminating unnecessary jargon, convoluted sentences, and complex structures, writers can make their work more accessible, engaging, and impactful. In this chapter, we will explore various techniques that can help improve the quality of your writing, enabling you to connect with your readers on a deeper level.

Know your audience:

Understanding who you are writing for is crucial. Tailor your language, tone, and style to suit the intended readership. By adopting a reader-centric approach, you can eliminate jargon and use language that resonates with your target audience. This ensures your message is clear and easily comprehensible.

Simplify your sentences:

Long, convoluted sentences can confuse and deter readers. Break down complex ideas into succinct and straightforward sentences. Aim to convey one idea per sentence, and use punctuation effectively to avoid run-on sentences. Clear and concise sentences not only enhance readability but also improve overall comprehension.

Use plain language and avoid jargon:

Jargon can alienate readers unfamiliar with specific terms or ideas. Replace industry-specific terminology with simpler, universally understood language. While some technical writing may require the use of niche vocabulary, it is essential to explain these terms in plain language to ensure clarity. This approach fosters inclusivity and broadens your readership's understanding.

Focus on active voice and strong verbs:

Active voice not only adds clarity but also contributes to concise and engaging writing. Sentences in the active voice are direct, vigorous, and easier to follow. Similarly, using strong verbs instead of weak ones brings vitality and precision to your writing. This technique enables readers to connect with your message more effectively.

Break down complex ideas:

When dealing with complex ideas, break them down into smaller, more digestible sections. Use headings, bullet points, or subheadings to organize information and provide clarity. Additionally, incorporate relevant examples, analogies, or metaphors to make abstract concepts more relatable and understandable.

Structure your writing logically:

Ensure the logical flow of your ideas by organizing your writing in a coherent way. Open your piece with a clear introduction, followed by well-structured paragraphs that build on each other. Each paragraph should present a single idea or argument. Use transition words to create smooth connections between paragraphs and maintain a cohesive structure.

Edit and revise rigorously:

The importance of editing and revising cannot be overstated. After completing a draft, review it critically to eliminate any unnecessary or convoluted content. Focus on simplifying language, eliminating redundancy, and ensuring logical coherence. Involve others for feedback, as they can provide fresh perspectives and identify areas that need improvement.

By using these techniques, you can enhance the clarity and simplicity of your writing, thus making it more accessible, engaging, and impactful for your readers. Remember to know your audience, simplify sentences, avoid jargon, use active voice and strong verbs, break down complex ideas, structure your writing logically, and carefully edit and revise your work. Ultimately, effective writing hinges on the ability to communicate ideas with clarity and simplicity while forging a connection with your readers.

DEVELOPING YOUR UNIQUE WRITING VOICE TO CAPTIVATE READERS & ESTABLISH A STRONG AUTHORIAL PRESENCE:

As writers, our ultimate goal is to captivate readers and establish a strong authorial presence. But how can we achieve this? Developing a unique writing voice is the key. It lets us incorporate our personality and tone into our writing, making it distinct and engaging. In this article, we will explore strategies to uncover your individual writing style, creating works that resonate with readers and leave a lasting impression.

Embrace your personality:

To develop your unique writing voice, start by embracing your personality. Reflect on what makes you different and what experiences have shaped you. Your individuality will infuse your writing with authenticity, making it relatable and engaging for readers. Don't be afraid to let your quirky humor, deep introspection, or unique perspective shine through in your writing.

Read extensively:

Reading is a fundamental part of finding your writing voice. Explore various genres, styles, and authors. Study their techniques, but avoid copying their voices. Instead, examine how their writing resonates with you and what parts you appreciate. Over time, you'll discover different elements that appeal to you, letting you incorporate them seamlessly into your own work.

Experiment with different writing exercises:

Conducting writing exercises will help you explore different writing styles and tones. Experiment with various prompts, genres, and literary devices. For example, try writing a scene in different tones, such as humorously, solemnly, or romantically. By pushing your limits and stepping out of your comfort zone, you'll uncover new facets of your writing style to incorporate into your unique voice.

Identify your target audience:

Understanding your target audience is crucial in developing your writing voice. Consider who you want to read your work and tailor your writing. What tone, language, and themes would resonate most with your desired readers? By aligning your writing with their preferences, you can better establish your authorial presence and connect with your audience on a deeper level.

Write regularly:

The more you write, the better you'll understand your writing voice. Make writing a habit and set aside dedicated time to practice and experiment. Over time, you will discover patterns, preferences, and strengths within your writing. Embrace those qualities, polish them, and make them the foundation of your unique voice.

Seek feedback and revise:

Sharing your work with others and seeking constructive feedback is essential for growth as a writer. Allow others to evaluate your voice and style objectively. Their insights may help you uncover blind spots or areas where you can improve. Remember, constructive criticism is an opportunity for growth, not an attack on your unique voice. Embrace it, reflect on it, and revise.

Developing your unique writing voice requires a combination of self-reflection, exploration, and practice. Embrace your personality, read extensively, experiment with different writing exercises, identify your target audience, write regularly, and seek feedback. By incorporating elements of your personality, tone, and experiences, you can captivate readers, establish a distinctive authorial presence, and leave a lasting impact with your writing. Embrace the journey of discovering your unique writing voice, and let it guide your pen toward success.

HARNESSING THE POWER OF VIVID IMAGERY & SENSORY LANGUAGE THAT RESONATES WITH YOUR AUDIENCE:

Harnessing the power of vivid imagery and sensory language is crucial in creating a reading experience that resonates with your audience. By using descriptive language, metaphors, and sensory details, writers can paint a vivid picture in the minds of their readers, evoking emotions and engaging their senses.

When incorporating descriptive language, it is important to appeal to all the senses - sight, sound, smell, taste, and touch. By doing so, you can transport your readers into the world you are creating, making them feel as if they are experiencing it firsthand. For example, instead of simply stating that the room was dark, you could describe it as "a dimly lit room, with shadows clinging to the corners like ghosts, and the only source of light being a flickering candle that cast eerie dances on the cracked walls."

Metaphors, on the other hand, help to engage the readers' imagination by comparing two seemingly unrelated things. They offer a fresh perspective and let readers see things in a new light. For example, instead of saying someone was "angry," you could say "a storm brewed inside him, thunder echoing in his voice, and lightning crackling in his eyes."

Sensory details play a significant role in immersing readers in your writing. By vividly describing the smells, sounds, and textures of a scene, you evoke a deeper connection with your audience. For example, instead of mentioning that it was raining, you could describe "the raindrops falling like a symphony on the rooftop, their pitter-patter creating a soothing melody that whispered through the open windows."

Discovering your unique writing voice is an ongoing process that involves understanding your own personality, perspectives, and beliefs. Through the exploration of these elements you can establish a writing style authentic to you. Whether it is your sense of humor, your observations about life, or the way you perceive the world, incorporating these parts into your writing helps create a strong authorial presence.

One strategy to uncover your writing style is by experimenting with different writing techniques and genres. By trying out various approaches, you can discover what resonates most with you and lets you express yourself authentically. Reflecting on your personal experiences and emotions can also be a powerful way to infuse your writing with depth and honesty.

Another important part of developing your writing voice is understanding the tone you want to convey to your readers. By consciously choosing the mood of your writing, whether it be humorous, somber, or suspenseful, you can create an emotional connection with your audience. This emotional resonance helps captivate readers and keeps them engaged throughout your work.

By harnessing the power of vivid imagery, sensory language, and metaphors, writers can create an immersive reading experience for their audience. Additionally, by uncovering and incorporating their unique writing style, personality, and tone, writers establish a strong authorial presence that captivates readers and invites them to connect on a deeper level.

MASTERING THE ART OF STORYTELLING TO CREATE COMPELLING & ENGAGING STORIES THAT CAPTIVATE READERS FROM BEGINNING TO END:

Storytelling is an age-old craft that has captivated audiences for centuries. Whether it be through books, movies, or even oral traditions, the art of storytelling has the power to transport us to different worlds, evoke emotions, and leave a lasting impact. In this section, we will delve into the mastery of storytelling, exploring various narrative techniques such as plot development, character building, and creating tension. By understanding these techniques, writers can create compelling and engaging stories that captivate readers from beginning to end.

Plot Development:

One of the key elements of a captivating story is a well-developed plot. A plot serves as the blueprint that guides the narrative, presenting a sequence of events that unfold throughout the story. To create a compelling plot, writers must consider the elements of conflict, rising action, climax, and resolution.

By introducing a central conflict, writers create tension and intrigue, propelling the story forward. This conflict can take many forms - from external battles to internal struggles within characters' minds. A plot should have a carefully structured rising action that keeps readers engaged as the tension gradually builds toward the climax - the most intense and pivotal moment of the narrative. Finally, a satisfying resolution should tie up loose ends and provide closure to the story, leaving the reader fulfilled.

Character Building:

Character development is another crucial part of storytelling that draws readers in. Strong, relatable, and compelling characters can breathe life into a narrative, letting readers form emotional connections and invest in their journeys. To achieve this, writers must carefully craft their characters by considering their backgrounds, motivations, flaws, and desires.

By providing characters with distinct personalities and complex dynamics, writers can create conflict and tension between them, further driving the plot forward. Additionally, characters should experience growth and change throughout the story, ensuring their development feels organic and believable.

Creating Tension:

Tension is a vital element that can keep readers hooked and eager to turn each page. It can be achieved through various narrative techniques such as foreshadowing, pacing, and the strategic use of suspense. By gradually building tension, writers can create anticipation and keep readers engaged.

Foreshadowing, or subtly hinting at future events, can create a sense of unease or curiosity. Pairing this with carefully timed revelations can add depth to the story and keep readers on the edge of their seats. Pacing involves controlling the speed at which events unfold - combining moments of calm with intense action or conflict to create a rollercoaster effect. Last, strategic use of suspense, such as cliffhangers or unanswered questions, can compel readers to keep reading to discover what happens next.

Mastering the art of storytelling requires a deep understanding of narrative techniques such as plot development, character building, and creating tension. By honing these skills, writers can create compelling and engaging stories that captivate readers from beginning to end. Remember, a well-developed plot, complex and relatable characters, and carefully crafted tension can elevate a story, leaving a lasting impact on its audience. So, dive into storytelling and unleash your creativity to craft narratives that will transport and captivate readers for generations to come.

RHYTHM AND FLOW TO CAPTURE THE READER'S ATTENTION & KEEP THEM ENGAGED THROUGHOUT YOUR WORK:

Rhythm and flow are the magical elements that can transform a piece of writing into an extraordinary experience for the reader. Like the beat of a song, the sentence structure, pacing, and dialogue within a text create a symphony of words that captures the reader's attention and keeps them engaged from start to finish. The delicate balance of these components allows for a smooth and harmonious reading experience.

Sentence structure plays a vital role in establishing the rhythm of a piece. Short and punchy sentences can create a sense of urgency, driving the narrative forward and building suspense. But longer, more complex sentences can lend a lyrical quality to the prose, giving it an elegant and melodic tone. By using a variety of sentence lengths and structures, writers can maintain a dynamic pace, keeping the reader captivated throughout.

Pacing is the heartbeat of a story, dictating the speed at which events unfold and emotions are conveyed. Like a symphony conductor, the writer must carefully control the pace, ensuring it aligns with the desired effect. Quick, snappy pacing may be appropriate for action-packed scenes or thrilling moments, while slower pacing might build tension or convey introspective moments. By skillfully manipulating the pacing, the writer can create a visceral experience, evoking different emotions and captivating the reader's attention.

Dialogue, often touted as the "music of language," is another essential element in establishing rhythm and flow. Dialogue breathes life into characters and provides an opportunity for them to interact with each other and the reader. Through dialogue relationships are forged, emotions are revealed, and conflicts are resolved. Well-crafted dialogue not only advances the plot but also adds a natural ebb and flow to the narrative, enhancing the overall rhythm of the piece.

To create a smooth and harmonious reading experience, writers must master the art of balancing these elements. A text that flows seamlessly from one sentence to the next, with punctuated pauses and energetic bursts, dances like a well-choreographed performance. It grabs the reader's attention and urges them to keep turning the pages.

Attention to sentence structure, pacing, and dialogue is crucial in maintaining the reader's engagement. A monotonous rhythm or lack-luster pacing can lull the reader into a state of disinterest, causing them to lose focus and connection with the story. Conversely, a well-constructed rhythm and seamless pacing can immerse the reader in the narrative, making the text almost impossible to put down.

Rhythm and flow are the invisible threads that bind a piece of writing, breathing life into it and captivating the reader's attention. The careful consideration of sentence structure, pacing, and dialogue creates a symphony of words that harmonizes to deliver a smooth and engaging reading experience. By understanding the importance of these elements and practicing their manipulation, writers can create works that resonate deeply with their audience, leaving a lasting impact.

EDITING AND REVISING LIKE A PRO TO IMPROVE THE OVERALL QUALITY & IMPACT OF YOUR WRITING:

Editing and revising are crucial steps in the writing process that can transform a mediocre piece into an outstanding one. However, many writers struggle with these stages, unsure of where to start or how to improve their work effectively. In this guide, we will share practical tips to help you self-edit, proofread, and revise your writing like a professional. By implementing these strategies, you can refine your language, tighten your prose, and eliminate unnecessary repetitions, ultimately enhancing the overall quality and impact of your writing.

Take a break before editing:

Once you finish writing, set your work aside and take a break before diving into the editing process. This break lets you detach yourself from the piece, helping in assessing it objectively. By approaching your writing with fresh eyes, you'll spot errors, inconsistencies, and areas that require improvement more effectively.

Review for content and structure:

Before focusing on refining language, make sure your piece has a strong foundation. Read through your work and evaluate the overall structure, making sure your ideas flow logically and meaningfully. Look for any gaps in information, inconsistencies in argumentation, or potential areas where further elaboration may be necessary. By refining the core structure, you'll set a solid base for the subsequent editing and revising process.

Cut unnecessary repetitions:

Repetitions weaken your writing and make it less engaging. Scan your work for instances where you've unintentionally repeated concepts, phrases, or ideas. Delete these repetitions, and find alternative ways to convey your message more succinctly. This step improves the clarity of your writing, making it more concise and impactful.

Eliminate excessive modifiers:

While adjectives and adverbs are useful for descriptive purposes, excessive use can dilute your prose and make it less powerful. Review your work to identify instances where modifiers could be eliminated or replaced with stronger nouns or verbs. This practice strengthens your writing and enables readers to visualize scenes vividly without relying heavily on excessive description.

Seek clarity through concise language:

Effective writing is concise and clear. Evaluate each sentence, aiming to convey your message with few words. Eliminate unnecessary words, phrases, or jargon that may hinder understanding. Replace wordy expressions with more precise and straightforward ones, focusing on delivering your ideas crisply. This approach enhances the readability and impact of your writing.

Proofread with precision:

Proofreading is an essential step to catch any lingering errors, such as typos, grammatical mistakes, or punctuation errors. Read your work slowly and carefully, paying attention to each word and sentence. Use grammar and spell-checking tools, but don't only rely on them. Print your work or read it aloud, as this helps in identifying errors that may have been overlooked on a screen. Remember that proofreading isn't about fixing errors; it's also an opportunity to fine-tune your writing further.

Editing and revising are vital to improving the overall quality and impact of your writing. By following these practical tips, you can refine your language, tighten your prose, and eliminate unnecessary repetitions. Remember to take breaks, evaluate your content and structure, cut repetitions, eliminate excessive modifiers, seek clarity through concise language, and proofread meticulously. With these strategies, you'll develop the skills of a pro-editor and elevate your writing to new heights.

EMBRACING EXPERIMENTATION AND CONTINUOUS IMPROVEMENT IN ORDER TO EVOLVE & PERFECT YOUR WRITING STYLE OVER TIME:

Embracing experimentation and continuous improvement are cornerstones of honing one's craft as a writer. Encouraging writers to explore different writing styles, genres, and techniques is pivotal in their growth and development. By venturing beyond their comfort zones and trying new approaches, writers expand their creative horizons and enrich their writing prowess.

Understanding that finding one's unique writing style takes time, writers must emphasize the importance of continuous practice. As a musician or an athlete needs consistent training to improve their skills, writers need to consistently practice writing to refine their craft. Establishing a regular writing routine helps cultivate discipline and creates opportunities for exploration and growth.

Feedback plays an instrumental role in a writer's journey toward improvement. It is crucial to foster an environment where writers feel comfortable sharing their work openly, receiving constructive criticism, and engaging in insightful discussions. Constructive feedback helps writers identify their strengths and weaknesses, and provides guidance for their future endeavors. Peer workshops, writing circles, and collaborating with fellow writers are effective ways to yield diverse perspectives and invaluable insights.

In the pursuit of perfecting one's writing style, the process of refinement is indispensable. Encouraging writers to constantly revise, edit, and polish their work instills a sense of meticulousness and attention to detail. Through constant refinement, writers mold their words to create captivating narratives, vivid descriptions, and engaging dialogues that captivate readers.

Ultimately, embracing experimentation and continuous improvement enables writers to evolve and refine their writing style. It encourages them to step outside their creative comfort zones, explore a myriad of genres and writing techniques, and embrace diverse perspectives. By highlighting the importance of continuous practice, feedback, and refinement, writers can embrace their journey, nurture their talents, and ultimately unlock their full potential as masterful storytellers.

Chapter Summary:

Chapter 11 delves into the art of impactful writing. It emphasizes the importance of simplicity and clarity, advising writers to avoid complex language, break down intricate concepts, and ensure coherency for effective communication.

It encourages individuality in writing by incorporating personal elements that reflect the writer's unique identity. The chapter highlights immersive writing techniques such as vivid imagery, sensory words, and metaphors that help paint vivid pictures in the reader's mind.

It also suggests structuring a captivating story with an exciting plot, relatable characters, and engrossing tension. Attention is drawn to the significance of rhythm and flow in the narrative, suggesting a mix of short and long sentences for pacing and authentic dialogue for engagement.

The chapter concludes by underlining the critical role of editing and revising in enhancing the final output. Writers are urged to scrutinize their work for structural coherence, redundancy, clarity, and grammatical accuracy, ensuring their writing leaves a memorable impression.

· · ·

In our Next Chapter...

Dive into the transformative world of editing and revising with Chapter 12, your indispensable roadmap to elevate your written masterpiece from good to phenomenal. This chapter reveals the magic behind successful self-editing techniques. It encourages breaks, advocates for reading aloud, simplifies the intricate, and guides you in gathering invaluable feedback.

Shine a light on your plot's consistency, breathe life into your characters, and perfect your story's pacing. Discover the untapped potential of professional editing and discover how it can redefine your work!

Navigating the editing landscape can challenge, but Chapter 12 will equip you with the right strategies to overcome these hurdles. Learn to spot and fill plot holes, bid farewell to repetitive phrases, and maintain a harmonious writing style that resonates with your readers.

Unearth the power of story mapping, infuse your language with diversity, and ensure your writing aligns with your personal style guide. The final section of this enlightening chapter will inspire you to fine-tune your final drafts, incorporating constructive feedback, authenticating dialogues, and perfecting your work's visual aesthetics.

As our journey in Chapter 12 concludes, remember that the secret ingredient to creating a masterpiece is patience coupled with an unwavering attention to detail. Embrace this journey and let your writing shine!

~

EDITING AND POLISHING: A STEP-BY-STEP GUIDE TO SELF-EDITING & WORKING WITH PROFESSIONAL EDITORS TO REFINE YOUR MANUSCRIPT

UNDERSTANDING THE IMPORTANCE OF EDITING & ITS IMPACT ON REFINING THE MANUSCRIPT TO ITS FULLEST POTENTIAL:

EDITING IS an essential step in the writing process that often goes overlooked or underestimated. It is the process of revising and polishing a manuscript to ensure its quality and coherence. While writing provides the foundation for a piece, editing plays a crucial role in refining the manuscript to its fullest potential. The term editing encompasses various parts such as proofreading, content revision, grammar correction, and improving overall readability.

One of the primary reasons editing is significant is because it lets writers eliminate errors and inconsistencies. Often, while engrossed in writing, authors may overlook or miss minor mistakes such as typos, punctuation errors, or grammatical inaccuracies. Editing provides an opportunity to correct these errors, allowing the writing to be error-free and more professional.

Editing lets writers improve the overall clarity and coherence of their work. During the writing process, it is common to have gaps in information, unclear statements, or disorganized thoughts that may confuse readers. By revisiting the manuscript and editing it, writers can make sure the content flows logically, ideas are effectively conveyed, and any ambiguities or contradictions are resolved. This enhances the readability and comprehensibility of the text, making it more enjoyable and engaging for the audience.

Additionally, editing lets writers evaluate the effectiveness of their content and make necessary revisions. By reviewing their work objectively, authors can identify gaps in information, weak arguments, or irrelevant sections that may detract from the overall strength of the manuscript. Then writers can revise and restructure their content to ensure it aligns with their original intention and goals. This process often involves deleting unnecessary information, adding relevant details, or rearranging sections for a more cohesive outcome.

Editing also plays a vital role in upholding the writer's voice and maintaining consistency throughout the piece. It makes sure the chosen tone, style, and perspective remain consistent, providing a unified reading experience for the audience. Without proper editing, the writer's voice may become diluted or fragmented, leading to a lack of coherence and authenticity.

Editing is an indispensable part of the writing process that helps refine a manuscript to its fullest potential. It eradicates errors and inconsistencies, enhances clarity and coherence, evaluates content effectiveness, and maintains consistency in the writer's voice. Embracing the importance of editing lets writers maximize the impact and quality of their work, ensuring they deliver a polished and refined manuscript that captivates their readers.

SELF-EDITING TECHNIQUES: PRACTICAL TIPS & STRATEGIES FOR AUTHORS TO EFFECTIVELY SELF-EDIT THEIR WORK:

Self-Editing Techniques:

Effective self-editing is crucial for authors to refine their work and ensure its quality. Here are practical tips and strategies to help you improve your self-editing skills and produce polished writing:

Take a break: Before diving into the editing process, step away from your work for a while. This break lets you approach your writing with fresh eyes, making it easier to spot errors and inconsistencies.

Read aloud: Reading your work aloud is an excellent way to identify awkward sentence structures, repetitive phrasing, and grammar errors. It helps you catch mistakes that might have gone unnoticed while silently reading.

Print it out: Viewing your writing on paper can help you notice errors missed on a screen. Mark up the printed version by underlining or highlighting problem areas that need attention.

Check for grammar and spelling errors: Carefully proofread your work to ensure correct grammar and spelling. Use spell-check and grammar-check tools, but be cautious as they might not catch all mistakes. Rely on your own knowledge and consult grammar style guides where required.

Simplify sentence structure: Complex sentence structures can hinder clarity and flow. Consider breaking long sentences into shorter ones to improve readability. Look for unnecessary repetition and fillers that can be eliminated without changing the message.

Examine word choice: Evaluate the word choices in your writing to enhance clarity and precision. Avoid overusing certain words or clichés. Look for stronger, more specific alternatives that convey your ideas with greater impact.

Trim excessive language: Eliminate unnecessary words and phrases, especially redundancies and wordy constructions. Aim for concise writing that is clear and to the point. Be on the lookout for filler words like "very," "just," or "really" that can often be omitted without changing the meaning.

Improve paragraph transitions: Ensure your paragraphs flow smoothly from one to the next. Use transitional words and phrases, such as "however," "in addition," or "on the contrary," to help readers follow your train of thought and maintain coherence.

Verify logical consistency: Check that your ideas and arguments are logically presented and supported throughout your piece. Look for any gaps, inconsistencies, or contradictions in your writing and address them.

Seek feedback: Consider sharing your work with trusted friends, colleagues, or writing groups for constructive criticism. Other perspectives can offer valuable insights and help you identify areas that need improvement.

Read professionally edited works: Regularly expose yourself to well-edited writing to refine your own editing skills. Pay attention to how professionals address grammar, sentence structure, clarity, and flow. This exposure can help you develop a better sense of what quality writing looks like.

Self-editing is an ongoing practice, and it becomes easier with experience. By implementing these techniques, you can consistently produce work that is refined, coherent, and engaging, ultimately enhancing your writing abilities.

THE ART OF REVISING FOR PLOT CONSISTENCY, CHARACTER DEVELOPMENT, & PACING:

Revising is an essential step in the journey of creating any written work. It lets writers refine their ideas and ensure their manuscripts are polished and engaging. When revising, one must delve into the intricate details of the story, carefully assessing areas that require further development or restructuring. This section will explore the art of revising, focusing on techniques to enhance plot consistency, character development, and pacing within a manuscript.

· · ·

Plot Consistency:

Plot consistency refers to the coherence and flow of the events in a story. When revising, pay attention to the overall plot structure and make sure each scene, chapter, and subplot aligns seamlessly. To achieve plot consistency:

- Review the cause-and-effect relationships between events. Check if each action is a logical consequence of a previous event.

- Assess the clarity of the story's conflicts and resolutions. Make sure conflicts are compelling and their resolutions are satisfying.

- Avoid plot holes or inconsistencies by identifying any contradictions or unexplained actions. Continuity is crucial in creating a believable narrative.

Character Development:

Characters are the heart of any story. Revision offers an opportunity to deepen their personalities and make them more relatable and dynamic. Consider these aspects when revising for character development:

- Ensure that characters' actions, choices, and dialogue are consistent with their established traits. Characters should evolve throughout the story, but changes must be motivated and consistent.

- Assess if each character has their own distinct voice, mannerisms, and motivations, enabling readers to connect with them on an emotional level.

- Examine character arcs and growth. Characters should face challenges, transform, and learn from their experiences. Revising lets you refine their journeys.

Pacing:

Pacing is the rhythm and tempo of a story. It determines the speed at which events unfold and influences the reader's engagement. When revising for pacing:

- Evaluate the balance between action, dialogue, and introspection. Different scenes may require varying amounts of each but be mindful of maintaining a good pace throughout.

- Consider the length of scenes and chapters. Long, detailed scenes may slow down the story, while shorter ones can create a sense of urgency. Vary the length strategically based on the desired impact.

- Use transitions effectively to maintain a smooth flow. Transitions can accelerate or decelerate the pace, depending on the scene's purpose.

The art of revising is a meticulous process that lets writers refine their manuscripts. By focusing on plot consistency, character development, and pacing, writers can ensure their stories are compelling and engaging to readers. Through careful revision, writers bring their manuscripts closer to their full potential, crafting a captivating narrative that resonates with their audience.

SEEKING PROFESSIONAL EDITING ASSISTANCE: CHOOSING THE RIGHT EDITOR FOR YOUR NEEDS

Writing a manuscript or any piece of written work is a laborious and intricate process. Often, writers invest substantial time and effort into crafting their work, but their efforts may go unnoticed if the text is riddled with errors and lacks coherence. This is where professional editors play a pivotal role. They have the expertise to refine and polish your manuscript, ensuring it reaches its full potential. In this section, we will discuss the benefits of working with professional editors and the various types of editing services available. Additionally, we will provide guidance on how to find and select the right editor to suit your needs.

Benefits of Professional Editors:

Objective Evaluation: Professional editors offer a fair perspective on your work. They bring fresh eyes to your manuscript and provide constructive feedback on its strengths and areas that need improvement. This helps authors to objectively assess their writing and make necessary revisions.

Enhanced Coherence and Flow: Editors specialize in enhancing the readability and overall flow of your work. They can identify and rectify issues related to organization, structure, and clarity, making sure the reader can effortlessly navigate through your ideas.

Grammar and Language expertise: no matter how skilled a writer you are, it is easy to miss grammar mistakes and punctuation errors. Professional editors have a keen eye for such mistakes and can polish your grammar, syntax, and punctuation, resulting in a polished and error-free final product.

Tailored Industry Standards: Editors know publishing industry standards, ensuring your work meets the expected criteria and guidelines. They can help you adhere to the specific requirements of your target audience or publishing platform.

Types of Editing Services:

Developmental Editing: This type of editing focuses on the overall structure, content, and organization of your work. Editors provide feedback on plot development, character consistency, pacing, and other crucial parts. Developmental editing helps authors shape ideas, refine storylines, and strengthen the overall impact of their writing.

Copyediting: Copyediting involves a detailed review of grammar, spelling, punctuation, sentence construction, and overall language usage. Editors make sure the author's intended message is clear and concise while maintaining the author's unique voice. Copyediting focuses on improving the technical parts of the writing to enhance its readability.

Proofreading: Proofreading is the final stage of editing, primarily focusing on catching typographical errors, misspellings, and minor formatting issues. A proofreader makes sure the text is error-free and ready for publication.

Finding the Right Editor:

Research: Look for professionals who specialize in your genre or subject matter. Research their credentials, experience, and earlier client testimonials to understand their suitability for your project.

Samples and Testimonials: Request samples of their previous work or ask for recommendations from authors who have worked with them. This lets you evaluate their style, editing approach, and overall competence.

Communication and Collaboration: Engage in open communication with potential editors. Discuss your project, timelines, and expectations to ensure you are on the same page. A good editor should be responsive, receptive to your ideas, and able to provide constructive feedback.

Budget and Pricing: Consider your budget and assess the pricing models offered by different editors. Some charge per word, per hour, or have fixed rates. Choose an editor who offers a suitable pricing structure without compromising on quality.

Compatibility: It is important to find an editor whose communication style and editing philosophy align with yours. Building a good rapport will help with a productive and harmonious editing process.

Working with professional editors offers many benefits, including objective evaluation, improved coherence, polished language, and adherence to industry standards. By understanding the different types of editing services available, you can select the most appropriate one for your needs. By conducting thorough research, evaluating samples, communicating effectively, considering your budget, and ensuring compatibility, you can find the right editor to help you refine and enhance your written work, preparing it for its intended audience.

COLLABORATING WITH EDITORS:

Collaborating with editors is crucial for any writer. Working together harmoniously can lead to the enhancement of the story, improved clarity, and a polished final product. Here are insights and strategies on effectively collaborating with editors:

Establish clear communication: Open and transparent communication is the foundation of a successful collaboration. Make sure you and your editor are on the same page regarding expectations, deadlines, and guidelines for the project. Ask questions and seek clarification when needed to avoid any misunderstandings.

Provide necessary background information: Editors may not be familiar with the intricacies of your story or subject matter. You will provide them with the necessary background information to help them understand the context. This could include relevant research material, previous drafts, or any additional resources that can help in their understanding of the topic.

Be open to constructive feedback: Embrace constructive criticism as an opportunity to grow as a writer. Editors are there to help enhance your work, not tear it down. Approach feedback with an open mind and consider it as a valuable chance to improve your writing. Remember, constructive feedback highlights areas that can be strengthened, and it should not be taken personally.

Engage in a collaborative dialogue: Establish a collaborative relationship with your editor by fostering a dialogue rather than a one-sided interaction. Share your thoughts, concerns, and ideas while being receptive to their suggestions and insights. This open dialogue can lead to a deeper understanding of the story and better collaboration.

Respect editorial decisions: Editors have specific expertise and a keen eye for what works best in a piece of writing. While it's essential to voice your opinions, it is equally important to respect their editorial decisions. Trust their judgment and be willing to compromise when necessary for bettering the final version.

Meet deadlines and be proactive: To maintain a smooth collaboration, meet agreed-upon deadlines and communicate any potential delays in advance. Being proactive and organized will foster a productive working relationship with your editor.

Maintain professionalism: Always maintain a professional tone and demeanor while interacting with your editor. Treat them with respect, respond promptly to their queries, and be professional in your written and verbal communication. This will help create a positive working environment that benefits both parties.

Collaborating effectively with editors requires clear communication, providing necessary background information, embracing constructive feedback, engaging in collaborative dialogue, respecting editorial decisions, meeting deadlines, and maintaining professionalism. Embrace the collaboration as an opportunity to improve your work and produce the best outcome.

ADDRESSING COMMON EDITING CHALLENGES: PRACTICAL SOLUTIONS & TECHNIQUES TO OVERCOME THESE CHALLENGES.

Editing is an essential part of the writing process that helps authors polish their work and ensure its effectiveness. However, several common challenges often arise during the editing stage. In this article, we will address three of these challenges: identifying and resolving plot holes, eliminating repetitive phrases, and ensuring consistency in voice and tone. Additionally, we will provide practical solutions and techniques to overcome these challenges.

Identifying and Resolving Plot Holes:

Plot holes can undermine the coherence and believability of a story. To identify plot holes, reread your work carefully and try to approach it with a fresh perspective. Here are techniques to help resolve plot holes:

Create a timeline: Map out the chronological order of events in your story to ensure consistency. This will help you identify any inconsistencies or gaps that need to be addressed.

Seek feedback: Share your work with beta readers or writing groups. Their fresh eyes can often spot plot holes you might have missed.

Ask questions: Put yourself in the reader's shoes and ask yourself questions about the story. This will help expose gaps in logic or missing information that need to be filled.

Use storyboarding: Visualize your story's events using a storyboard or a flowchart. This can reveal any missing plot points or illogical sequences.

Eliminating Repetitive Phrases:

Repetitive phrases can make writing sound monotonous and uninteresting. Here are techniques you can use to eliminate repetitive phrases:

Use a thesaurus: When you notice yourself using the same word or phrase multiple times, consult a thesaurus to find alternative terms that convey the same meaning.

Focus on variety: Ensure you vary the sentence structures and lengths throughout your writing. This can help avoid repetitive sentence patterns.

Edit with fresh eyes: Take a break from your writing and revisit it later with a fresh perspective. This will make it easier to spot repetitive phrases you may have become blind to.

Ensuring Consistency in Voice and Tone:

Consistency in voice and tone is crucial for maintaining the overall atmosphere and engaging the readers. Here are techniques to ensure consistency:

Develop a style guide: Create a style guide that outlines the preferred tone, voice, and writing style for your work. Refer to this guide during the editing process to maintain consistency.

Track changes: Use the track changes feature in word processing software to keep track of your revisions and make sure voice and tone remain consistent throughout.

Read aloud: Read your work aloud to identify any inconsistencies in voice and tone. This can help you detect jarring shifts or deviations from your intended style.

Editing challenges such as identifying and resolving plot holes, eliminating repetitive phrases, and ensuring consistency in voice and tone can be overcome with practical techniques. By applying these solutions and taking a methodical approach to editing, authors can enhance the overall quality and coherence of their work. Remember to be patient and open to feedback, as editing is an iterative process that ultimately leads to a stronger final piece.

POLISHING THE FINAL DRAFT:

Congratulations! You've made it to the final stage of polishing your manuscript. In this phase, we will walk you through the steps you need to take to ensure your work is in its best shape before it goes out into the world. Let's get started!

Implement Suggested Edits:

Go through all the feedback you received, whether from beta readers, critique partners, or editors. Evaluate each suggestion carefully and make the necessary changes. Remember, you have the final say in what stays and what goes, but be open to constructive criticism that could improve your work.

Fine-Tune Dialogue:

Dialogue is a crucial part of any story. It lets readers connect with your characters and adds depth to your narrative. Take the time to read through your dialogue carefully, making sure it sounds authentic and serves a purpose. Pay attention to realism, character voice, and pacing. Consider reading the dialogue aloud or asking someone to read it to you to ensure it flows naturally.

Enhance Descriptive Language:

Creating vivid and engaging descriptions is key to immersing readers in your story. Look closely at your descriptive passages and make them come alive. Use sensory details to evoke emotions and paint a clear picture in the readers' minds. Be cautious not to overdo it, as balance is important. Aim for descriptive language that enhances the atmosphere and adds value to the overall story.

Ensure Formatting and Style Consistency:

Formatting and style consistency might not be the most glamorous part of the process, but it's crucial for a professional-looking manuscript. Pay attention to font, font size, indents, line spacing, and chapter headings. Consistency in these elements will make your manuscript seem polished and easy to read. Additionally, double-check that you are following the industry-standard formatting guidelines, especially if you plan to submit your work to publishers or literary agents.

Perform a Final Read-Through:

Before you hit that publish or submit button, take the time to perform a final read-through of your manuscript. This step is essential to catch any lingering errors, such as typos, grammar mistakes, or weak sentences. Read your work slowly, line by line, and give it the attention it deserves. Try to distance yourself from the story to approach it with fresh eyes. Consider hiring a professional proofreader or using editing software to help eliminate any last-minute errors.

Taking the time to polish your manuscript is crucial for presenting your best work to the world. While it may be tempting to rush the final stages, resist the urge and give your manuscript the attention it deserves. By implementing suggested edits, fine-tuning dialogue, enhancing descriptive language, ensuring formatting and style consistency, and performing a final read-through, you'll make sure your book is ready to captivate readers and make a lasting impression.

Chapter Summary:

It might feel like a lot but take your time. Your work's worth it, and with patience and these handy tips, you'll have something you can be really proud of.

Chapter 12 delves into the crucial task of editing and revising a manuscript, highlighting its importance in making good writing great.

It provides an insightful guide on self-editing techniques, encouraging taking breaks, reading aloud, simplifying complex parts, and seeking feedback from trusted sources.

Emphasis is placed on ensuring plot consistency, authentic character development, and ideal pacing, alongside the potential benefits of professional editing help.

The chapter also offers advice on choosing the right editor and fostering effective collaboration with them. It acknowledges the challenges faced during editing such as finding plot holes, eliminating repetitive phrases, and maintaining a consistent writing style.

To address these, it suggests strategies like story mapping, introducing variety in language, and using a style guide.

The final section motivates writers to polish their final drafts, considering feedback received, authenticating dialogues, and ensuring visual aesthetics through appropriate font, size, and spacing.

The chapter concludes, underscoring the value of patience and meticulous attention to detail in creating a piece of writing to be proud of.

In our Next Chapter...

Immerse yourself in Chapter 13, where we delve into the heart of nonfiction storytelling: the creation of full-blooded, compelling characters.

This chapter provides invaluable guidance on portraying your characters in their full complexity. Learn how to imbue your writing with sensory and emotional richness, letting readers empathize deeply with your characters.

Understand the importance of character evolution, mirroring real-life growth and transformation. Not just the protagonist, but also the significance of supporting characters is highlighted, adding to your story's depth and realism.

Chapter 13 is a must-read for writers striving to make their non-fiction narratives resonate with readers, long after they've turned the last page.

CREATING MEMORABLE CHARACTERS AND PERSONALITIES: HOW TO BRING THE INDIVIDUALS IN YOUR NONFICTION STORY TO LIFE & ENGAGE READERS THROUGH THEIR EXPERIENCES

THE IMPORTANCE OF DEVELOPING WELL-ROUNDED CHARACTERS & HOW IT CONTRIBUTES TO ENGAGING READERS ON A DEEPER LEVEL:

IN THE REALM of nonfiction storytelling, the importance of developing well-rounded characters cannot be overstated. While nonfiction narrative often focuses on recounting true events and conveying factual information, including memorable characters adds depth, relatability, and emotional connection that engages readers on a deeper level. Characters bring stories to life; their experiences, personalities, and growth provide a lens through which readers can immerse themselves in the narrative, creating a lasting impact.

One of the primary reasons for developing well-rounded characters in nonfiction storytelling is the ability to humanize real-life events and ideas. Nonfiction often examines complex subjects like history, culture, or social issues. By introducing relatable characters, readers are provided with a real representation of these abstract ideas. Characters act as anchors, letting readers perceive the story through their perspectives, helping with empathy and understanding.

Well-developed characters enhance the credibility and authenticity of nonfiction storytelling. These individuals become conduits for conveying information and ideas. Through their personal experiences, characters add a layer of personalization and detail that cannot be achieved through factual reports alone. Rather than presenting a barrage of data, characters lend a unique human touch that invites readers to connect emotionally with the story.

In addition, well-rounded characters contribute to the overall engagement of readers. The more invested readers become in the characters, the more they become invested in the story itself. Characters with distinct personalities, motivations, and conflicts captivate readers, provoking curiosity and prompting them to follow the narrative from start to finish. This engagement enables readers to form an emotional bond with the characters, resulting in a more impactful reading experience.

Developing well-rounded characters in nonfiction storytelling allows for the exploration of broader themes and ideas. By mapping character arcs and growth, authors can tackle complex subjects from a personal perspective, making the information more accessible and relatable. Through the lens of characters, readers can see how abstract ideas like resilience, love, or social change manifest in real life, reinforcing the significance of these themes.

Ultimately, including well-rounded characters in nonfiction storytelling is essential to create memorable narratives that resonate with readers on a deeper level. By humanizing ideas, enhancing credibility, fostering engagement, and exploring broader themes, characters enrich the nonfiction experience. As readers relate to and empathize with the trials and triumphs of these characters, they form connections that extend beyond the final pages, leaving a lasting impact on their minds and hearts.

IDENTIFYING KEY TRAITS & MOTIVATIONS OF THE INDIVIDUALS IN YOUR NONFICTION STORY, ALLOWING READERS TO CONNECT WITH THEM EMOTIONALLY:

To identify and understand the unique personalities and motivations of the individuals in your nonfiction story, ensuring readers can connect with them emotionally, follow these guidelines:

Conduct thorough research: Start by gathering as much information as possible about each individual. Read books, articles, or any material that relates to their life, experiences, and achievements. Contact people who have interacted closely with them, such as family members, friends, or colleagues, to gain insights into their character traits, motivations, and personal stories.

Analyze their actions and behaviors: Study the actions and behaviors of the individuals closely. Look for patterns or consistent traits that emerge. Do they have a relentless drive for success, or are they motivated by a deeper purpose? Are they introverted or extroverted? Observing how they interact with others and navigate various situations can provide valuable clues about their personalities and motivations.

Explore their background: Delve into their upbringing, cultural background, and significant events that shaped them. Consider how these factors may have influenced their personality development and motivated them to pursue certain goals or aspirations. Understanding their background lets you explain their behavior and provide context for their actions, making them more relatable to readers.

Seek unique perspectives: Try to find multiple perspectives on the individual, not just the popular or widely acknowledged ones. This can help paint a more comprehensive picture of their personality. Diverse viewpoints provide a depth and authenticity that resonates with readers, enabling them to connect emotionally with the individuals in your story.

Highlight personal anecdotes or stories: Humans are inherently attracted to personal stories and anecdotes. By incorporating such details into your narrative, you can humanize the individuals and offer glimpses into their lives, making them more relatable. These stories can emphasize their motivations, struggles, and triumphs, creating an emotional connection for readers.

Use direct quotes and descriptions: When possible, incorporate direct quotes from interviews or conversations with the individuals themselves. This lets readers hear their voices and understand their thoughts and emotions more intimately. Combine these quotes with descriptive language to vividly portray their personality, mannerisms, and motivations.

Consider their impact on others: Assess the impact the individuals have had on the lives of those around them. How do they inspire, motivate, or influence others? Understanding their role in the lives of people connected to them offers valuable insights into their character and motivation, enabling readers to form a connection based on shared emotions and experiences.

Stay objective and avoid oversimplification: While it is essential to identify key traits and motivations, remember to remain objective and avoid oversimplification. Humans are complex beings, and reducing them to a single feature or motive can diminish their depth. Capture the nuances of their personalities and motivations by presenting a well-rounded and balanced portrayal.

By implementing these guidelines, you can effectively identify and understand the unique personalities and motivations of the individuals in your nonfiction story. This understanding will help readers connect with them emotionally, fostering an engaging and meaningful reading experience.

USING VIVID DESCRIPTIONS AND SENSORY DETAILS TO BRING CHARACTERS TO LIFE, ENABLING READERS TO VISUALIZE & EXPERIENCE THEIR EXPERIENCES:

Using descriptive language and sensory details is a powerful tool in bringing characters to life and enabling readers to visualize and experience their experiences. It is through such vivid writing that readers can immerse themselves in the story and form a deep connection with the characters.

Descriptive language uses words that appeal to the senses, such as sight, sound, smell, taste, and touch. By painting a visual picture in the reader's mind, the characters become more real and relatable. For example, instead of simply saying a character has brown hair and blue eyes, the author might describe the character's hair as a rich chestnut brown, cascading in gentle waves down their back, and their eyes as a piercing sapphire blue, sparkling with intelligence. Such details not only make the character more vibrant but also let readers feel a sense of familiarity. They can visualize someone in their own life who has similar features and connect emotionally with the character.

Sensory details go beyond visuals and add depth to a character's experiences. Using the other senses, such as sound, smell, taste, and touch, the author helps readers engage more fully with the story. For example, describing the sound of a character's laughter as infectious, joyous, and filled with warmth creates an auditory image that evokes emotions within the reader. Similarly, describing the smell of freshly baked cookies wafting through the air, the taste of a warm cup of cocoa on a cold winter's day, or the touch of a soft breeze against a character's skin engages readers on a sensory level, letting them experience the same sensations.

Descriptive language and sensory details also help to reveal a character's personality and emotions. When a character's experiences are vividly described, readers can empathize and understand them better. For example, describing a character's trembling hands, racing heartbeat, and sweat-soaked clothes during a moment of intense fear or anxiety helps readers feel the same emotions the character is experiencing. This makes the character more relatable and the story more immersive.

Using descriptive language and sensory details is highly effective in bringing characters to life and enabling readers to visualize and experience their experiences. By painting a vivid picture in the reader's mind and appealing to their senses, characters become more real, relatable, and emotionally engaging. Descriptive language and sensory details create a deep connection between the readers and the characters, making the reading experience all the more immersive and memorable.

SHOWCASING CHARACTER GROWTH AND TRANSFORMATION TO MAKE THE STORY MORE RELATABLE & CAPTIVATING FOR READERS.

Character growth and transformation are crucial elements in storytelling that add depth and complexity to a narrative. Portraying character development and personal growth throughout the story not only makes it more relatable but also captivates readers by letting them connect with the characters on a deeper level.

When a character undergoes growth and transformation, they evolve from their initial state, adopting new beliefs, behaviors, and perspectives. This transformation can be driven by various factors such as a life-altering event, a personal realization, or the influence of other characters.

One of the primary reasons character growth is significant is that it mirrors real-life experiences. As readers, we often go through our journey of personal growth and self-discovery. By seeing a character facing challenges and overcoming them, we draw parallels to our own struggles and triumphs. This relatability lets readers emotionally invest in the story, forging a connection between themselves and the characters.

Character growth brings authenticity and believability to a story. Imagine a protagonist who remains stagnant throughout the narrative, unchanged by their experiences. That character would lack depth and fail to engage the reader's interest. But a character who undergoes growth becomes multi-dimensional, as they grapple with their flaws, face obstacles, and ultimately transcend their limitations. This transformation makes the character's journey more believable and captures the reader's attention, making them eager to see the character's evolution.

Character growth and transformation also contribute to the overall plot progression. As a character changes, their choices, interactions, and decisions impact the events unfolding within the story. These transformations create a ripple effect, changing the dynamics between characters, introducing new conflicts, and propelling the plot forward. This interplay between character development and story progression adds depth, complexity, and intrigue to the narrative, keeping readers engaged and eager to discover what happens next.

In addition, character growth lets readers witness the triumph of the human spirit. When characters overcome their flaws or learn from their mistakes, it instills hope and inspiration in readers. It emphasizes the universal truth that change is possible, and that growth is an inherent part of the human experience. This hope not only captivates readers but also leaves a lasting impact, encouraging self-reflection and personal growth in their own lives.

Ultimately, showcasing character growth and transformation is essential in making a story relatable and captivating for readers. By letting them connect with the characters on an emotional level, inspiring hope and showing the power of change, authors create narratives that resonate deeply with their audience. Through compelling character arcs, writers elevate their storytelling, creating tales not only entertaining but also transformative.

INCORPORATING DIALOGUE AND INTERACTION BETWEEN CHARACTERS, ILLUSTRATING THEIR RELATIONSHIPS & ENHANCING THE AUTHENTICITY OF THEIR EXPERIENCES:

Title: A Night at the Coffee Shop

INT. COFFEE SHOP - NIGHT

CLAIRE, a middle-aged woman with a warm smile, enters the coffee shop. She looks around, searching for her old friend, JANE, an independent and ambitious woman in her early thirties.

. . .

CLAIRE

(smiling)

Jane! Over here!

JANE

(excitedly)

Claire! It's been ages! How have you been?

They hug tightly, showing their deep bond.

CLAIRE

(sincerely)

I've missed you, Jane. Life's been a rollercoaster. How about you?

JANE

(chuckling)

Same here, Claire. Let's grab a coffee and catch up.

They order their drinks and sit comfortably at a cozy corner table.

CLAIRE

(teasingly)

So, any romantic escapades lately?

. . .

JANE

(raising an eyebrow)

You know me too well, Claire. There was someone, but it didn't work out. Just wasn't meant to be.

CLAIRE

(supportive)

Ah, the rollercoaster of relationships. We've all been there. Don't worry, Jane, your perfect match is out there somewhere.

They share a warm smile as they sip their coffees.

JANE

(grateful)

You always know how to boost my spirits, Claire. So, tell me about your job. You're a renowned psychologist now, right?

CLAIRE

(modestly)

Well, renowned might be an exaggeration, but yes, I've been working hard in the field. It's tough, Jane, but incredibly rewarding. The stories I hear daily remind me of the beauty and fragility of the human experience.

JANE

(sincerely)

I'm so proud of you, Claire. Your dedication and empathy have always inspired me. You make the world a better place.

Claire blushes and glances at her watch hesitantly.

CLAIRE

(apologetically)

I wish I could stay longer, but I have another appointment soon. How about we plan a longer catch-up next time?

JANE

(grinning)

Deal! We'll make it an all-day affair. I've missed these heart-to-heart conversations, Claire.

They exchange genuine smiles and stand up for a final, tight hug.

CLAIRE

(whispering)

You mean the world to me, Jane. Stay strong, and remember I'm always just a call away.

JANE

(teary-eyed)

Thank you, Claire. Our friendship means everything to me too. Take care, always.

. . .

They say their goodbyes and part ways, both touched by the authenticity and power of their connection.

FADE OUT.

BALANCING STRENGTHS AND WEAKNESSES ADD COMPLEXITY & DEPTH TO YOUR CHARACTER'S PERSONALITIES WHILE KEEPING THEM RELATABLE TO READERS:

Portraying characters with a mixture of strengths and weaknesses is vital to creating complex and relatable personalities. Such characters not only add depth to a story but also engage readers on a more profound level. In literature, characters who are too perfect or completely flawed can be difficult to connect with. However, by balancing strengths and weaknesses, authors can humanize their characters and make them relatable to readers.

One of the primary reasons for incorporating a mix of strengths and weaknesses is to ensure a certain level of believability. Real people are not without flaws, and neither should fictional characters be. When a character has flaws, it lets readers identify with them on a personal level because imperfections are a part of the human condition. By acknowledging their weaknesses, characters become more relatable, and readers can see themselves in their struggles and their growth.

Portraying characters with a mix of strengths and weaknesses adds complexity to their personalities. Showing a character's strengths lets them excel in certain areas and display admirable qualities. Whether it's intelligence, bravery, or charisma, these strengths make the character stand out and become someone readers can admire or look up to.

However, it is the character's weaknesses that truly add depth and complexity. These weaknesses can be internal struggles, such as personal insecurities or emotional baggage, or external challenges, like physical limitations or moral conflicts. By highlighting these flaws and obstacles, authors introduce opportunities for character development and growth throughout the narrative.

When a character faces challenges and makes mistakes due to their weaknesses, it becomes an opportunity for readers to see their humanity. This not only makes the character more relatable but also creates tension and conflict within the story. The character's strengths may lead them to success, but their weaknesses can lead to failure or compel them to make difficult choices.

Additionally, balancing strengths and weaknesses allows for dynamic relationships between characters. When different characters have complementary strengths and weaknesses, they can support or challenge each other. This interaction between characters adds further complexity and keeps the narrative engaging.

Balancing strengths and weaknesses in characters is crucial for creating complexity and depth in their personalities while keeping them relatable to readers. Acknowledging flaws and imperfections humanizes characters, letting readers connect with them on a personal level. By showcasing strengths, characters become admirable, while their weaknesses provide opportunities for growth and development. This nuanced portrayal adds layers of complexity to the story and helps with dynamic relationships between characters. Ultimately, a mix of strengths and weaknesses helps authors create well-rounded and relatable characters that resonate with readers.

CREATING MEMORABLE SUPPORTING CHARACTERS IN YOUR NONFICTION STORY, EXPLORING THEIR UNIQUE ROLES AND CONTRIBUTIONS TO THE NARRATIVE, & DEMONSTRATING THEIR IMPACT ON THE MAIN CHARACTERS' EXPERIENCES.

In any nonfiction story, supporting characters play a critical role in bringing depth and authenticity to the narrative. While the main characters may take center stage, the supporting characters often leave a lasting impression on readers. They not only add richness to the story, but also contribute to the main characters' experiences in profound ways.

One of the key reasons for developing compelling supporting characters is to create a diverse and relatable cast that mirrors reality. These characters help paint a broader picture of the world being portrayed, providing different perspectives, backgrounds, and personalities. By doing so, readers can engage with a variety of voices and experiences, making the story more inclusive and fascinating.

Supporting characters serve as catalysts for the main characters' growth and transformation. They generate conflict, challenge beliefs, and offer guidance, pushing the main characters beyond their limits. Think of the wise mentor, the unexpected ally, or the formidable antagonist – each member of the supporting cast has a unique role to play in shaping and influencing the journey of the main characters.

The impact of supporting characters on the main characters' experiences cannot be overstated. Through their interactions, the main characters undergo new challenges, confront their flaws, and come to epiphanies that propel the story forward. Supporting characters are often responsible for imparting wisdom, providing comic relief, or unveiling hidden truths, which significantly shape the main characters' worldview and change the trajectory of their story.

For example, in a memoir about overcoming personal struggles, a supporting character could be a close friend who offers unwavering support during the protagonist's darkest moments. This friend's unwavering faith and encouragement contribute to the protagonist's resilience and determination to overcome their obstacles. Without this character, the readers might not fully appreciate the protagonist's journey and the significance of their triumph.

Additionally, supporting characters can help humanize the main characters, showing their vulnerability, strengths, and flaws. By developing deep bonds with the main characters, these supporting characters become a powerful tool for converting a two-dimensional lead into a fully fleshed-out individual. They bring out various emotional parts of the main characters, showcasing their layers and complexity.

The significance of developing memorable supporting characters in nonfiction stories cannot be understated. These characters present diverse perspectives and experiences, enhancing the authenticity of the narrative. They play crucial roles in shaping the main characters' journeys, providing catalysts for growth, and affecting their lives in profound ways. By crafting compelling supporting characters, authors create a multi-dimensional and captivating storytelling experience that resonates with readers far beyond the pages of the book.

Chapter Summary:

Chapter 13 emphasizes the importance of creating vivid, multi-dimensional characters in nonfiction.

It guides writers to explore a character's personality, history, and motivations, using descriptive writing that immerses the reader in their senses and emotions.

Characters are not to be oversimplified; they need to showcase complexities, strengths, weaknesses, and evolve over the story's course, reflecting our own life transformations.

The chapter also highlights the role of supporting characters in contributing to the story's depth and realism. A character's growth, transformation, and interaction with others create a relatable, captivating narrative that resonates with readers long after they've finished reading.

In our Next Chapter...

In Chapter 14 the significance of creating powerful endings to shape the reader's overall experience is underscored.

Discover how an effective conclusion can enhance the reader's connection to the story, providing closure and evoking strong emotions.

This chapter emphasizes that the ending serves as the author's final opportunity to leave a lasting impression, addressing lingering questions and reaffirming the story's key themes. Beware of the dangers of a poor ending, as it can diminish an otherwise captivating narrative, leaving readers unsatisfied.

Explore the role of supportive characters in non-fiction works. Learn how their varied viewpoints enrich the story, driving the growth of the main characters.

Delve into a wide range of techniques for crafting effective endings. From resolving conflicts and tying up loose ends to providing closure and eliciting emotions, this chapter offers valuable insights and practical advice.

The art of balancing these parts is crucial to creating a profound impact that resonates with the reader long after the book is closed.

Discover how careful consideration of each element makes sure the story lingers in the hearts and minds of readers.

Embark on a journey through the art of crafting influential endings in Chapter 14 of "Constant: The Art of Storytelling." Uncover the secrets to leaving a lasting impact, captivating readers until the very end.

CHAPTER FOURTEEN

CRAFTING POWERFUL ENDINGS: UNDERSTANDING THE IMPORTANCE OF A STRONG CONCLUSION & LEAVING A LASTING IMPRESSION ON YOUR READERS

THE SIGNIFICANCE OF A STRONG CONCLUSION IN A BOOK, & HOW IT CAN MAKE OR BREAK THE OVERALL READING EXPERIENCE FOR THE AUDIENCE:

A STRONG CONCLUSION in a book holds immense significance, as it has the power to make or break the overall reading experience for the audience. The conclusion serves as the final imprint left on the readers' minds, sealing their opinions and emotions regarding the story. It is the author's last opportunity to leave a lasting impression.

One of the primary purposes of a strong conclusion is to provide closure. After investing time and emotions into a book, readers seek resolution and a sense of satisfaction. A weak or rushed conclusion can leave them feeling unfulfilled, resulting in a negative reading experience. But a well-crafted conclusion offers closure to various plotlines, addresses lingering questions, and ties up loose ends, leaving the reader with a sense of completion.

Additionally, a strong conclusion has the potential to evoke strong emotions and leave a profound impact on the audience. It can elicit feelings of joy, sadness, surprise, or even contemplation. By providing a memorable ending, authors can leave their readers pondering the story's themes or even reconsidering their own beliefs and perspectives. This emotional resonance enhances the reading experience and solidifies the book's significance in the readers' minds.

A strong conclusion can also help reinforce the book's overarching message or theme. By revisiting and reinforcing the central ideas explored throughout the narrative, the author leaves readers who clearly understand the story's purpose. This reinforces the book's value and makes sure readers take away important lessons or insights, further enhancing the overall reading experience.

Conversely, a weak conclusion can undermine the impact of even the most compelling narrative. It can dampen the readers' enthusiasm, leave significant plotlines unresolved, or fail to provide closure, leaving them dissatisfied and potentially questioning the overall quality of the book. A weak conclusion may also diminish the value of the story's themes, failing to leave a lasting impression or encourage readers to reflect on the book's core ideas.

In nonfiction storytelling, developing compelling supporting characters is essential for creating a well-rounded and engaging narrative. These characters play unique roles and contribute to the story, amplifying the overall reading experience.

First, supporting characters allow for a deeper exploration of different perspectives and experiences within the nonfiction story. By providing alternative viewpoints, supporting characters challenge the assumptions and beliefs of the main characters, prompting them to grow and evolve throughout their own narrative arcs. This adds depth and complexity to the overall story, enabling readers to gain a multifaceted understanding of the topic.

Supporting characters often serve as catalysts for the main characters' growth and development. Through their interactions and relationships, supporting characters can drive the plot forward, present new challenges, or offer guidance and support. Their impact on the main characters' experiences helps shape their journey, making it more dynamic and engaging for the readers.

Supporting characters also add richness and texture to the nonfiction story. Their unique backgrounds, personalities, and stories create a tapestry of human experiences that mirror the diversity of the real world. By including a diverse range of supporting characters, authors can provide readers with a more comprehensive and relatable reading experience, enabling them to connect with the characters and the narrative on a deeper level.

A strong conclusion in a book holds immense significance as it can make or break the overall reading experience for the audience. It provides closure, evokes powerful emotions, reinforces the story's themes, and leaves a lasting impact on the readers. Similarly, compelling supporting characters in nonfiction storytelling contribute to the narrative by offering different perspectives, catalyzing growth in the main characters, and adding richness and complexity to the story. Their unique roles and contributions enhance the readers' overall experience and make the nonfiction story more engaging and memorable.

EXPLORING VARIOUS TECHNIQUES TO CREATE POWERFUL ENDINGS, SUCH AS RESOLVING CONFLICTS, TYING UP LOOSE ENDS, AND PROVIDING CLOSURE TO CHARACTERS & STORYLINES.

One of the most important parts of any story is its ending. A powerful ending can leave a lasting impact on readers or viewers, solidifying their emotional connection to the narrative. It is the culmination of all the events and character arcs, and it should provide resolution, closure, and satisfaction to the audience. In this section, we will explore various techniques that can help create powerful endings.

Resolving conflicts: Many stories revolve around conflicts and obstacles that the characters must overcome. So, resolving these conflicts in a satisfying way is crucial for a powerful ending. This can be done by having the protagonist face their final and most significant challenge, leading to a resolution true to the story's themes and messages. It is important to ensure that the resolution feels earned and not forced, as that can weaken the impact of the ending.

Tying up loose ends: Throughout a story, there are often minor plot threads or unanswered questions that intrigue the audience. Tying up these loose ends can provide a sense of closure and fulfillment. It can be done by explaining unresolved mysteries, resolving incomplete character arcs, or revealing the fate of supporting characters. However, it is essential to balance closure and leaving room for the audience's imagination, as an overly neat ending can feel unrealistic or unsatisfying.

Providing closure to characters: Characters are at the heart of any story, and their arcs greatly contribute to its emotional impact. So, giving each character a meaningful conclusion is essential for a powerful ending. This can be achieved by showcasing their personal growth, resolving internal conflicts, or letting them achieve their goals or find redemption. By satisfying the audience's investment in the characters, the ending becomes more impactful and memorable.

Resolving storylines: In addition to characters, a story often consists of multiple interwoven storylines. Address all pertinent storylines and provide closure to each one. This can be done by making sure all significant plot points are resolved, conflicts are settled, and story arcs are completed. By doing so, the audience feels a sense of satisfaction and fulfillment, knowing that every narrative element has been addressed and accounted for.

Evoking emotions: A powerful ending should evoke a strong emotional response from the audience. This can be achieved through various means such as an unexpected twist, a poignant revelation, or a bittersweet conclusion. By provoking emotions, the ending lingers in the minds and hearts of the audience, leaving a lasting impact.

Creating a powerful ending requires careful consideration of various techniques. By effectively resolving conflicts, tying up loose ends, providing closure to characters, resolving storylines, and evoking emotions, an ending can leave a lasting impression on readers or viewers. Remember, a powerful ending is not just about closure, but also about making the story resonate long after the final page or scene.

UNDERSTANDING THE EMOTIONAL IMPACT OF A WELL-CRAFTED ENDING, AND HOW IT CAN RESONATE WITH READERS LONG AFTER THEY FINISH THE BOOK:

A well-crafted ending has the power to leave an indelible emotional impact on readers long after they have read a book. It takes skill and finesse to create a conclusion that resonates deeply with the audience, encapsulating their journey and leaving them with a lasting impression. By understanding the emotional impact of a well-crafted ending, authors can leave their readers reflecting, contemplating, and even yearning for more.

One of the key aspects of an emotionally impactful ending lies in its ability to evoke a strong emotional response. Whether it is joy, sadness, anger, or a myriad of other emotions, the ending should strike a chord deep within the reader's heart. This emotional resonance occurs when the story's climax aligns with the reader's expectations and desires. Through this alignment a sense of fulfillment or catharsis is achieved, confirming the reader's investment in the narrative.

A well-crafted ending also has the power to leave readers pondering the themes, ideas, and lessons explored throughout the book. It lets them reflect on the characters' journeys and the growth they have seen. By highlighting the impact of these experiences, the ending can provoke introspection and ignite discussions on important topics. It prompts readers to look beyond the narrative, connecting the story to their own lives and experiences.

A strong ending can leave readers with a sense of closure, tying up loose ends and resolving conflicts. It provides a satisfying resolution, answering questions raised throughout the story. However, it is crucial to strike a delicate balance, as an ending that ties up every loose thread can feel too tidy and contrived. A well-crafted ending should leave room for interpretation, letting readers imagine the characters' futures and the potential continuation of their journeys beyond the pages of the book. [Ultimately, the emotional impact of a well-crafted ending lingers in the readers' minds long after they have put the book down. It sparks emotional connections, encourages reflection, and leaves an open invitation for readers to revisit the story in their thoughts and conversations. By carefully crafting an ending that resonates on a deep emotional level, authors can create a lasting and cherished bond between their readers and the narrative they have brought to life.

THE IMPORTANCE OF LEAVING A LASTING IMPRESSION ON READERS, AND HOW A MEMORABLE ENDING CAN LEAVE THEM PONDERING AND REFLECTING ON THE STORY'S THEMES & MESSAGES:

When it comes to storytelling, one part that often gets overlooked is the ending. Many writers focus so much on crafting compelling characters and engaging plotlines that they forget the importance of leaving a lasting impression on their readers. However, it is precisely the ending that can make or break a story's impact. A well-crafted and thought-provoking ending can leave readers pondering and reflecting on the story's themes and messages long after they have finished reading.

One reason why a memorable ending is essential is that it provides closure to the readers. Throughout the story, readers invest their time, emotions, and energy in following the journey of the characters. They become emotionally attached to the story's world and its inhabitants. The ending has the power to provide some resolution and tie up loose ends, helping readers find satisfaction and closure.

A memorable ending can also make readers reflect on the story's themes and messages at a deeper level. It is like a parting gift from the author, a final opportunity to leave readers with a profound thought or an impactful idea. When readers are left pondering the ending, they are more likely to revisit the story in their minds and engage in discussions about its meaning and significance. This reflection can lead to a deeper understanding of the story's core themes and encourage readers to think critically about the world around them.

Additionally, a memorable ending has the potential to create an emotional resonance that lingers. When a story ends on a powerful or emotionally charged note, it can evoke strong emotions in readers.

These emotions stick with them, letting the story become a part of their memories. This emotional connection becomes a lasting bond between readers and the story, making it more likely for readers to recommend it to others or revisit it.

However, creating a memorable ending is no easy task. It requires careful planning and consideration by the writer. One way to ensure a satisfying and impactful ending is to align it with the story's themes and messages. The conclusion should reflect and reinforce the story's central ideas, offering readers a sense of meaning and purpose. It should feel organic and authentic, giving readers a sense of fulfillment and resonance.

The importance of leaving a lasting impression on readers through a memorable ending cannot be overstated. The ending provides closure, helps readers reflect on the story's themes and messages, and creates an emotional resonance that lingers. By crafting an impactful and thought-provoking ending, writers can leave readers pondering and reflecting on the story long after they have turned the final page.

DIFFERENT TYPES OF POWERFUL ENDINGS THAT BRING ABOUT A SENSE OF CATHARSIS TO THOSE THAT PROVOKE THOUGHT & CONTEMPLATION:

Powerful endings in literature can have varying effects on readers. Some aim to provide a sense of catharsis, while others promote thought and contemplation. Let's explore different types of powerful endings and the impact they can have on readers.

Cathartic Endings: These endings provide a release of emotions, letting readers feel a sense of relief or resolution. They often tie up loose ends and offer a satisfying conclusion. Examples include the reconciliation between characters, the triumph of good over evil, or resolving a conflict. Such endings leave readers with a feeling of closure and a sense that justice or order has been restored.

Twist Endings: These endings surprise readers by subverting their expectations. Often seen in mystery or thriller genres, twist endings can shock, amaze, or leave readers questioning everything they thought they knew about the story. The sudden revelation of a hidden truth or an unexpected turn of events can provoke a strong emotional response, leaving readers in awe of the author's ingenuity.

Ambiguous Endings: Ambiguous endings intentionally leave aspects of the story unresolved or open to interpretation. They challenge readers to engage in deeper contemplation and make their own conclusions. These endings often prompt readers to reflect on the themes, motifs, and symbols presented throughout the narrative, inviting them to draw personal meaning from the story. Ambiguous endings can frustrate readers but also stimulate discussions and encourage readers to think critically about the text.

Bittersweet Endings: A bittersweet ending mixes elements of happiness and sadness. It creates a complex emotional experience by blending joy and sorrow, giving readers a nuanced perspective on the characters or the story's outcome. These endings acknowledge the complexities of life, where victories can come at a cost or where happiness can be tinged with sadness. Bittersweet endings resonate with readers who appreciate narratives that reflect the complexity of the human experience.

Open-Ended Endings: An open-ended ending deliberately avoids providing clear-cut answers or closure. It lets readers imagine possible outcomes or speculate about the future of the characters beyond the story's conclusion. Open-ended endings encourage readers to engage actively with the text and continue their own narratives in their minds. They can be thought-provoking, leaving readers contemplating the themes or moral dilemmas within the story long after they have finished reading.

Ultimately, powerful endings in literature can have different effects on readers. Whether they bring about catharsis, provoke thought, or leave room for interpretation, they enhance the overall impact of the narrative and provide a lasting impression.

CASE STUDIES AND EXAMPLES OF BOOKS WITH EXCEPTIONAL ENDINGS, ANALYZING WHAT MAKES THEM IMPACTFUL & HOW AUTHORS ACHIEVED THAT EFFECT:

Case Study 1: "Gone Girl" by Gillian Flynn

"Gone Girl" is a psychological thriller with a jaw-dropping ending that leaves readers shocked and in awe. The author, Gillian Flynn, masterfully crafts a narrative filled with twists and turns, ultimately leading to a conclusion that is both unexpected and satisfying.

What makes the ending of "Gone Girl" impactful is the clever use of unreliable narration throughout the book. Flynn skillfully manipulates the readers' perceptions by presenting two conflicting perspectives, leaving them questioning the truth of the story until the very end. The revelation of Amy Dunne's manipulative and sociopathic nature, and her intricate plan to frame her husband, Nick, is a true game-changer that catches readers off guard.

Flynn heightens the impact of the ending by building suspense gradually. She drops subtle hints and foreshadowing, engaging readers in a thrilling guessing game. By not revealing everything upfront, she keeps the readers hooked and invested in the story until the final pages. The sudden shift in power dynamics between the characters and the unexpected role reversals create an unforgettable climax that lingers long after the book is finished.

Case Study 2: "To Kill a Mockingbird" by Harper Lee

"To Kill a Mockingbird" is a classic novel that tackles themes of racial injustice and morality in a small Southern town. The ending of this book is both impactful and emotionally resonant, leaving a lasting impression on readers.

Harper Lee achieves this impact by creating a powerful juxtaposition between justice and injustice, hope and despair. The trial of Tom

Robinson, a black man falsely accused of rape, serves as the central conflict. Despite the evidence supporting Tom's innocence, the deeply rooted racism of the town leads to his unjust conviction. The readers see the heartbreaking aftermath of the trial as Tom is killed while trying to escape, symbolizing the loss of innocent lives in an unjust society.

Lee's writing style is raw and evocative, letting readers connect with the characters on a deep emotional level. The innocence and naivety of the protagonist, Scout, as she learns about the harsh realities of the world, makes the ending even more impactful. Through Scout's eyes, readers experience the bitter truth that justice doesn't always prevail.

The remarkable ending of "To Kill a Mockingbird" serves as a wake-up call, challenging readers to confront the injustices present in society and strive for a better future.

Exceptional book endings, like those found in "Gone Girl" and "To Kill a Mockingbird," rely on the element of surprise, the skillful development of characters, and exploration of thought-provoking themes. These authors successfully create unforgettable endings by defying expectations, delivering twists that challenge readers' preconceptions, and leaving them with a sense of lingering impact. Such outstanding endings captivate readers' minds, ignite emotions, and inspire contemplation long after the book is put down.

PRACTICAL TIPS AND EXERCISES FOR YOU TO IMPROVE YOUR UNDERSTANDING & EXECUTION OF POWERFUL ENDINGS, HELPING YOU CREATE MEMORABLE, SATISFYING CONCLUSIONS FOR YOUR STORIES:

Powerful endings can make or break a story. They leave a lasting impact on the reader and determine how they remember the entire narrative. As a writer, it is essential to master the art of crafting compelling endings that are both satisfying and memorable. Here are practical tips and exercises to help you improve your understanding and execution of powerful endings:

Understand the purpose of your ending: Ensure you clearly understand what you want to achieve with your ending. Do you want to leave readers feeling satisfied, shocked, or contemplative? Knowing your desired outcome will guide your writing process.

Study successful endings: Read books, short stories, or watch movies with powerful endings. Analyze how the authors or filmmakers created an impact through their conclusions. Consider elements like symbolism, payoff for character arcs, or unexpected plot twists that make those endings stand out.

Plan your ending in advance: It's crucial to have an ending in mind before you begin writing. Although your story might evolve as you write, having a destination in mind will help you structure your plot effectively and build tension toward the finale.

Foreshadow and build up to the ending: Create a sense of anticipation and build tension as you approach the conclusion. Drop subtle hints, foreshadow events, or provide clues throughout the narrative to keep readers engaged and guessing.

Resolve conflicts and tie loose ends: Ensure that major conflicts and storylines are resolved by the end. Leaving loose threads can be frustrating for readers, so provide closure for your characters and plotlines. However, leave room for a sense of wonder or possibility, as this can add depth to your ending.

Consider the emotional impact: Endings that leave a lasting impact often evoke strong emotions. Reflect on the emotions you want to elicit from your readers and find ways to resonate with them. Whether it's joy, sadness, or surprise, aim to evoke an emotional response that stays with your audience.

Experiment with different ending options: Try writing alternative endings to your story, exploring different possibilities. This exercise will help you evaluate the strengths and weaknesses of each option, letting you select the one that best serves your narrative.

Seek feedback from others: Share your draft endings with trusted writing partners, beta readers, or join writing communities to gather feedback. Others' perspectives can provide valuable insights into how effectively your ending resonates and whether it meets your intended goals.

Reflect on your favorite endings: Think about the stories that have left a lasting impact on you and analyze why their endings were so powerful. What made them memorable? What techniques did the writers employ? Reflecting on your favorite endings can inspire and inform your own writing style.

Revise and polish: Endings often require multiple revisions to ensure they achieve the desired impact. Take the time to refine your concluding chapter, paying attention to pacing, clarity, and emotional resonance. Each revision will bring you closer to the powerful ending your story deserves.

Powerful endings can elevate your storytelling and leave a lasting impression on your readers. With practice and dedication, you can master the art of crafting satisfying and memorable conclusions for your own stories.

Chapter Summary:

Chapter 14 underscores the significance of crafting influential endings to shape the readers' overall experience.

It states that an effective conclusion can enhance a reader's connection to the story, providing closure and eliciting strong emotions.

The chapter emphasizes that the ending is the author's final opportunity to make an impression, answer lingering questions, and reaffirm the story's key themes. It warns that a poor ending can diminish an otherwise compelling narrative, leaving readers discontented.

The chapter also touches on how supportive characters can enrich nonfiction, offering varied viewpoints and driving the growth of main characters.

Various techniques for effective endings, such as resolving conflicts, tying up loose ends, providing closure, and eliciting emotions, are discussed.

The chapter concludes by stating these parts must be balanced carefully to create a lasting impact, ensuring the story resonates with the reader long after the book is closed.

In our Next Chapter...

In the ever-evolving world of publishing, the journey doesn't end when your book hits the shelves. The success of any book relies heavily on post-publication strategies. Chapter 15 delves into this critical phase, offering a comprehensive guide on how to maintain the buzz around your book, maximize distribution channels, make sure your book stands out in a sea of competitors and cultivate beneficial relationships in the literary world.

You'll learn how to encourage readers to write reviews, keep the conversation going on social media, and even conducting book signings or talks. Explore ways to expand your book's reach by securing spots in online stores like Amazon, local bookshops, and even libraries. We'll walk you through the process of making your book visually appealing and easy to discover, discussing the importance of a captivating cover, accurate book details, and the power of good reviews.

This chapter emphasizes the importance of networking in the publishing industry. Discover how forging relationships with authors, agents, and professionals can amplify your book's promotion. Finally, we delve into evaluating your strategies - understanding what's working and what isn't, through sales analysis, online reputation management, and even direct surveys.

In Chapter 15, we break down the art of sustaining success in the simplest terms, making sure your book continues to reach readers long after its launch. Get ready to take your book promotion to the next level!

$\sim$

CHAPTER FIFTEEN

NAVIGATING THE PUBLISHING AND MARKETING PROCESS: EXPLORING TRADITIONAL PUBLISHING, SELF-PUBLISHING, & MARKETING STRATEGIES FOR SUCCESSFULLY LAUNCHING YOUR BOOK

TRADITIONAL PUBLISHING INDUSTRY, INCLUDING THE ROLE OF LITERARY AGENTS AND PUBLISHING HOUSES, AND THE BENEFITS AND DRAWBACKS OF PURSUING THIS ROUTE:

TRADITIONAL PUBLISHING REFERS to the traditional process of publishing books, which involves literary agents and publishing houses. Understanding the traditional publishing industry is crucial for authors looking to get their work published in this manner. In this article, we will explore the role of literary agents and publishing houses, as well as the benefits and drawbacks of pursuing this route.

The Role of Literary Agents:

Literary agents act as intermediaries between authors and publishing houses. They serve as a representative for authors, working to secure book deals and negotiate contracts on their behalf. Literary agents have in-depth knowledge of the publishing industry and can provide valuable guidance to authors, helping them navigate the complex publishing landscape. They often have established relationships with editors and publishers, letting them pitch manuscripts more effectively.

The Role of Publishing Houses:

Publishing houses are companies that specialize in publishing books. They play a crucial role in the traditional publishing process. Once a literary agent secures a book deal, the publishing house takes over and works closely with the author to edit, design, market, and distribute their book. Publishing houses have extensive resources and experienced staff to handle various parts of the book production process, ensuring a high-quality final product.

Benefits of Traditional Publishing:

Credibility and Prestige: Being published by a reputable publishing house lends credibility and prestige to an author's work. Traditional publishing often carries a certain level of validation and recognition in literary circles, which can help an author's career.

Editorial Support: Publishing houses have professional editors who work closely with authors to refine and polish their manuscripts. This editorial support makes sure the final product is of high quality and meets industry standards.

Marketing and Distribution: Traditional publishers have established marketing and distribution channels to reach a wide audience. They use their networks to promote books, arrange book tours, and secure bookstore placement, maximizing the exposure and potential sales of an author's work.

Drawbacks of Traditional Publishing:

Long Process: Traditional publishing generally involves a long process. From finding a literary agent to securing a book deal and going through editing and production, it can take several months or even years before a book is finally published.

Lack of Control: Once an author signs a publishing contract, they may have limited control over certain parts of their book, including cover design, title, and marketing strategy. Authors must collaborate and compromise with the publishing house.

Competition and Rejection: The traditional publishing industry is highly competitive, and rejection is common. Literary agents and publishing houses receive a vast number of submissions and can only accept a few manuscripts. Authors need persistence and resilience to navigate through rejection and find the right fit.

Understanding the traditional publishing industry is essential for authors considering this route. While it offers benefits such as credibility, editorial support, and extensive marketing resources, it also comes with drawbacks like a long and competitive process and a limited amount of control. Authors must carefully weigh the pros and cons to determine if traditional publishing is the right path for their book.

SELF-PUBLISHING OPTION FOR AUTHORS TO PUBLISH AND DISTRIBUTE THEIR BOOKS INDEPENDENTLY AND THE ADVANTAGES & CHALLENGES OF THIS APPROACH.

Self-publishing has become an increasingly popular option for authors who wish to have full control over the publishing process. With advancements in technology and the rise of digital platforms, authors now have the tools and platforms available to publish and distribute their books independently. In this article, we will explore the self-publishing option, including the various platforms and tools available to authors, and discuss the advantages and challenges of this approach.

First, let's discuss the platforms and tools that authors can use for self-publishing. One of the most well-known platforms is Amazon Kindle Direct Publishing (KDP). KDP lets authors upload their manuscripts, create book covers, set pricing, and make their books available for sale in e-book and print formats through Amazon's vast distribution network. Other popular platforms include Barnes & Noble Press, Smashwords, and Apple's iBooks Author.

Alongside these platforms, there are various tools available to help authors in the self-publishing process. Tools like Scrivener, Vellum, and Canva provide authors with the means to write, format, and design their books professionally. Editing and proofreading services, such as Reedsy, can also ensure the quality of the final product. Additionally, authors can leverage social media, blogs, and websites to promote their work and build a reader base.

Now, let's discuss the advantages of self-publishing. First, authors retain full control over their work, including creative decisions, pricing, and rights. Self-published authors have the freedom to write in any genre, experiment with different styles, and publish at their own pace. They also have the potential for higher royalty rates since they are not sharing profits with a traditional publisher.

Self-publishing can also offer faster publication times. While traditional publishing can take several years from the initial submission to seeing a book on store shelves, self-publishing lets authors release their work swiftly. This agility is especially beneficial for authors who want to capitalize on current trends or topics.

Self-publishing opens up opportunities for niche or specialized books that might not receive attention from traditional publishers. Authors can cater to specific audiences, provide valuable insights, and build a loyal readership within a specific genre or subject area.

However, self-publishing also presents several challenges. First, authors must take on all the responsibilities typically handled by a traditional publisher, including editing, cover design, formatting, and marketing. This requires a significant investment of time, effort, and potentially money, especially if authors choose to outsource certain tasks.

Another challenge is the lack of brand recognition and distribution networks that traditional publishers offer. Traditional publishers have established relationships with bookstores, libraries, and other retailers, making it easier for their books to reach a wider audience. Self-published authors often rely heavily on digital platforms, social media, and online promotions to gain visibility.

Additionally, self-published authors may face credibility challenges, as there is often a stigma attached to self-published works. Some readers may assume that self-published books lack quality and professional editing. To overcome this, authors must invest in professional editing, cover design, and effective marketing to ensure their books meet industry standards.

Self-publishing provides authors with the opportunity to publish and distribute their books independently. With various platforms and tools available, authors have the means to bring their creative visions to life. While self-publishing offers advantages such as creative control, potential higher royalties, and faster publication times, authors must also overcome challenges such as additional responsibilities, limited distribution networks, and credibility concerns. Ultimately, self-publishing can be a rewarding path for authors willing to invest their time, effort, and resources into creating and promoting their work.

THE IMPORTANCE OF EFFECTIVE MARKETING IN THE SUCCESS OF A BOOK & MARKETING STRATEGIES AUTHORS CAN EMPLOY:

Marketing plays a pivotal role in the success of a book by attracting readers' attention and generating interest. With the increasing competitiveness in the publishing industry, authors must use effective marketing strategies to ensure their books reach the intended audience. This section will highlight the significance of marketing in book success and discuss various strategies authors can use, including social media campaigns, book signings, and collaborations with influencers in the industry.

Creating Awareness through Social Media Campaigns:

Social media platforms have emerged as powerful tools for authors to connect with readers and promote their books. By leveraging platforms such as Facebook, Instagram, and Twitter, authors can create intriguing content, engage with potential readers, and generate awareness about their books. Through targeted ads, engaging posts, and interactive discussions, authors can build a loyal online community, thus maximizing the chances of book sales.

Amplifying Book Exposure through Book Signings:

Book signings provide authors with an excellent opportunity to connect with readers on a personal level while promoting their work. These events can be conducted in bookstores, libraries, or even online forums, allowing authors to not only sign copies but also engage in conversations with their readers. Book signings also help enhance the author's reputation and create a positive buzz around the book, attracting potential buyers and encouraging word-of-mouth recommendations.

Collaborating with Influencers in the Industry:

Collaborations with influencers, including book bloggers, booktubers, or established authors within the genre, can significantly boost the visibility and credibility of a book. These influencers already have a dedicated following of readers who trust their recommendations. By providing influencers with complimentary copies of the book, authors can leverage their reach and appeal to a broader audience. Positive reviews and endorsements from influencers can help establish a book's reputation and entice potential readers to buy it.

Leveraging Online Book Communities:

Participating in online book communities can help authors connect with like-minded readers and gain invaluable insights. Platforms such as Goodreads, Reddit's r/books, and various online book clubs create spaces for readers to discuss and recommend books they enjoy. Authors can actively engage in these platforms by participating in discussions, offering insights, and promoting their own work subtly. By establishing a strong presence within these communities, authors can tap into avid readers who actively search for new books to explore.

In today's competitive publishing landscape, effective marketing strategies are instrumental in achieving book success. Authors should embrace social media campaigns, book signings, collaborations with industry influencers and engagement in online book communities to generate awareness, boost book exposure, and ultimately entice readers to engage with their work. By adopting a comprehensive marketing approach and exploring these strategies, authors increase their chances of meeting their goals and connecting with a wider readership base.

BUILDING AN AUTHOR PLATFORM:

The idea of an author platform has become increasingly important in the digital age. In simple terms, an author platform refers to the author's online presence and their ability to attract and engage with their target audience. This platform serves as a way for authors to showcase their work, establish their brand, and ultimately, connect with readers.

Building a strong author platform is crucial for authors looking to expand their readership and gain visibility in a crowded publishing market. Here are practical tips and techniques to help authors build their platforms effectively:

Define your target audience: Understanding your target audience is the first step in building an author platform. Determine the demographics, interests, and preferences of your ideal readers, and tailor your platform accordingly. This will help you create content that resonates with your target audience and attracts their attention.

Build an author website: A well-designed and user-friendly website is a valuable asset for any author. Your website serves as a hub for your platform, providing essential information about you, your books, and upcoming projects. Include engaging content such as blog posts, book excerpts, and author interviews to keep visitors coming back.

Leverage social media: Social media platforms like Facebook, Twitter, Instagram, and LinkedIn are powerful tools for connecting with readers. Choose platforms that align with your target audience's preferences and invest time in building an authentic and engaging presence. Consistently share updates about your writing, interact with followers, and promote your work to expand your reach.

Create compelling content: To attract and engage readers, create valuable content beyond promoting your books. Share insights into your writing process, offer writing tips, and provide behind-the-scenes glimpses into your author journey. Additionally, consider guest blogging on industry-related websites or participating in author interviews to expand your reach.

Engage with your audience: Building an author platform is not just about showcasing your work; it's about creating meaningful connections with your readers. Respond to comments, messages, and emails promptly, and show genuine interest in your readers' opinions and feedback. Host virtual events, such as live Q&A sessions or book club discussions, to foster a sense of community and strengthen your bond with your audience.

Collaborate with influencers and book bloggers: Partnering with influential individuals in your genre or connecting with popular book bloggers can significantly boost your platform's visibility. Seek opportunities for guest posts, interviews, or joint promotions to tap into their established readership and gain exposure for your work.

Consistency is key: Building an author platform is a long-term endeavor, and consistency is crucial. Post regular updates, maintain an active presence on social media, and consistently provide valuable content to keep readers engaged. Establish a content calendar to help you plan and schedule your platform activities efficiently.

Building an author platform takes time and effort, but the benefits are well worth it. By strengthening your online presence, attracting readers, and engaging with your target audience, you'll create a solid foundation for your writing career and increase your chances of success in the competitive publishing industry.

BOOK LAUNCH STRATEGIES INCLUDING PRE-LAUNCH PROMOTION, MEDIA OUTREACH, AND LEVERAGING ONLINE PLATFORMS TO CREATE BUZZ & GENERATE INTEREST IN YOUR BOOK:

Launching a book is an exciting but challenging endeavor. To make sure your masterpiece receives the attention it deserves, it's crucial to implement effective book launch strategies. This guide aims to provide insights into these strategies, covering pre-launch promotion, media outreach, and leveraging online platforms to create buzz and generate interest in your book.

Understanding the Pre-Launch Phase:

Setting Goals: Define your goals, target audience, and desired outcomes to lay the foundation for a successful book launch.

Creating a Buzz: Learn techniques for building anticipation through teaser campaigns, engaging influencers, and using pre-launch promotions to generate excitement.

Identifying Key Platforms: Identify the platforms where your target audience gathers most frequently, ensuring your presence and message align with their interests.

Media Outreach Tactics:

Crafting a Compelling Press Release: Craft an attention-grabbing press release that highlights the unique parts of your book, enticing journalists and influencers to cover your story.

Building Relationships with the Media: Learn to build meaningful connections with journalists, bloggers, and influencers who cater to your target audience, increasing the likelihood of securing media coverage.

Media Kit Essentials: Understand the parts of a well-crafted media kit, including an author bio, book synopsis, sample chapter, endorsements, and high-quality visuals to maximize media attention.

Leveraging Online Platforms:

Captivating Author Website: Create a visually appealing website that showcases your book, provides information about your background, and engages readers with additional content.

Engaging Social Media Strategies: Learn to leverage different social media platforms effectively, including content creation tips, engagement techniques, and using social media advertising.

Blog Tours and Guest Posting: Explore the benefits of collaborating with influential bloggers and authors to expand your reach, establishing yourself as an authority in your genre.

Online Book Launch Events: Organize virtual events such as webinars, Q&A sessions, or live readings to engage your audience, generate interest, and help with book sales.

Post-Launch Strategies:

Gathering Reviews: Discover methods to encourage readers to leave reviews on influential platforms like Amazon, Goodreads, or book review blogs, enhancing your book's credibility.

Sustaining Momentum: Develop a plan to maintain the buzz created during the launch phase, including regular content creation and engagement with readers through newsletters or social media.

Expanding Promotion Efforts: Explore additional marketing tactics such as book signings, speaking engagements, podcast interviews, or collaborations with other authors to widen your book's exposure.

A successful book launch requires meticulous planning and strategic execution. By implementing the pre-launch promotion, media outreach, and leveraging online platforms, you can effectively generate buzz, expand your readership, and foster long-term success for your book. With the guidance provided in this book, watch your masterpiece soar to new heights of recognition and acclaim.

MAXIMIZING DISTRIBUTION CHANNELS TO OPTIMIZE BOOK AVAILABILITY & VISIBILITY IN THESE CHANNELS.

In today's digital age, authors have an array of distribution channels to choose from to reach readers worldwide. This section aims to discuss various distribution channels available to authors, including online retailers, brick-and-mortar stores, and libraries, and provides valuable insights on how to optimize book availability and visibility within each channel.

Online Retailers:

a. E-commerce platforms: Explore popular online marketplaces such as Amazon, Barnes & Noble, and Apple Books. Register as a publisher or self-published author to list your book.

b. E-book distribution platforms: Utilize platforms like Smashwords, Kobo, and Draft2Digital to distribute your e-book across multiple digital platforms, increasing your reach.

c. Author websites: Establishing an author website or blog provides a direct channel to promote and sell your books, as well as leverage social media to drive traffic to your online store.

Brick-and-Mortar Stores:

a. Independent bookstores: Target local independent bookshops, as they often support local authors and may be more willing to stock your book. Build relationships by attending events, signings, and fostering connections with store owners.

b. Chain bookstores: Approach major bookstore chains, such as Barnes & Noble, Books-A-Million, or Waterstones, to ask about their submission guidelines for including authors in their physical stores.

Libraries:

a. Public libraries: Collaborate with your local library to ensure your book is accessible to readers. Offer signed copies, donate copies to the library, or volunteer for book clubs and author discussions to raise awareness about your work.

b. Academic libraries: Explore opportunities to have your book stocked in university or college libraries to reach academic readers interested in your subject matter.

OPTIMIZING BOOK AVAILABILITY & VISIBILITY:

a. Metadata optimization: Pay close attention to metadata elements like title, author name, keywords, genre, and ISBN while publishing or listing your book. Accurate and relevant metadata helps readers discover your book during searches.

b. Professional cover design: Invest in a visually appealing and genre-appropriate book cover that grabs attention, as it plays a crucial role in attracting potential readers.

c. Book reviews and endorsements: Solicit reviews from trusted reviewers, book bloggers, or reputable review platforms. Positive reviews increase credibility, giving readers confidence to buy your book.

d. Social media and online promotion: Leverage social media platforms, author newsletters, and targeted advertising to promote your book, create an engaging author presence, and interact directly with readers.

e. Networking and collaborations: Join writing groups, author communities, and go to literary events to connect with fellow authors, agents, and industry professionals. Collaborations and cross-promotions can expand your audience.

Authors have a wealth of distribution channels at their disposal, enabling them to reach a broader audience. Using online retailers, engaging with brick-and-mortar stores, and actively involving libraries, authors can maximize their book availability and visibility. Implementing optimization strategies such as metadata refinement, professional cover design, securing endorsements, and harnessing the power of online promotion will further enhance an author's visibility and potential for success.

TRACKING AND EVALUATING MARKETING EFFORTS & ADJUSTING MARKETING TACTICS BASED ON THESE INSIGHTS.

Tracking and evaluating marketing efforts is crucial to determine the success of marketing campaigns and strategies. It helps businesses understand what is working well and what needs improvement. In this section, we will explore various methods to track and evaluate marketing efforts effectively.

Analyzing sales data: One of the most basic yet essential methods to track marketing success is through sales data analysis. By comparing sales data before and after implementing a marketing campaign, businesses can gauge the impact of their efforts on revenue generation. Important metrics to analyze include total sales, average order value, conversion rates, and customer acquisition costs. This data can highlight which channels, messages, or offers are driving sales and help refine future marketing strategies.

Tracking customer reviews and feedback: Customer reviews and feedback provide valuable insights into the effectiveness of marketing efforts. By tracking review platforms, social media channels, and customer surveys, businesses can gauge customer satisfaction, brand perception, and overall sentiment. Positive reviews indicate successful marketing engagement, while negative feedback may signal an area of improvement. Analyzing reviews can also help identify brand advocates and influencers who can be leveraged for future marketing campaigns.

Tracking website analytics: Website analytics tools such as Google Analytics provide a wealth of data to evaluate marketing efforts. By tracking metrics like website traffic, conversion rates, bounce rates, and time spent on site, businesses can assess the effectiveness of their website in driving engagement and conversion. Additionally, analyzing referral sources and user behavior on the website can reveal which marketing channels are driving the most valuable traffic.

Conducting surveys and focus groups: Surveys and focus groups let businesses gather direct feedback on marketing campaigns. By asking specific questions about awareness, recall, and effectiveness of the marketing messages, businesses can gain valuable insights into how their target audience perceives their efforts. These qualitative insights can help shape future marketing strategies and messaging.

Using social media listening tools: Social media listening tools let businesses track mentions and conversations about their brand or specific marketing campaigns across various social media platforms. By tracking sentiments, engagement levels, and reach, businesses can evaluate the success of their social media marketing efforts. These insights can help identify trends, popular topics, and customer preferences, informing future social media marketing tactics.

A/B testing: A/B testing is a method for comparing two different versions of marketing elements, such as ad copy, images, landing pages, or email subject lines. By randomly splitting the audience into two groups and exposing each group to a different version, businesses can determine which variation performs better in terms of engagement, click-through rates, or conversions. A/B testing provides data-driven insights to optimize marketing strategies and improve campaign effectiveness.

Tracking and evaluating marketing efforts are vital to make informed decisions and optimize marketing strategies. By analyzing sales data, tracking customer reviews and feedback, tracking website analytics, conducting surveys and focus groups, using social media listening tools, and conducting A/B testing, businesses can gain valuable insights to fine-tune their marketing tactics and ensure success.

Chapter Summary:

In Chapter 15, we explore the dichotomy of traditional and self-publishing. Traditional publishing provides credibility, professional editing, and marketing, but at the cost of control and a higher rate of rejection. On the other hand, self-publishing lets authors maintain control and potentially earn more, however, the responsibility for all tasks falls on the author. The key to choosing a path lies in the author's preferences and vision.

The chapter emphasizes the importance of marketing and maintaining an active online presence. Social media platforms like Facebook, Instagram, and Twitter are essential tools authors can use to engage with readers. In-person events like book signings and collaborations with influencers or book bloggers, can greatly increase a book's popularity.

As for post-launch strategies, authors should aim to keep the buzz alive, maximize distribution channels, invest in book aesthetics, network with industry professionals, and constantly review their strategies. This includes encouraging reviews on platforms like Amazon and Goodreads, ensuring the book is available on various platforms, creating an attractive cover, and tracking sales and online feedback.

∽

CONCLUSION

Nonfiction writing extends beyond simply stating facts; it aims to resonate with the target audience, evoke emotions, and offer a fresh perspective. This journey has explained the intricate process of nonfiction writing, shedding light on its nuances and the process of making your work accessible to the public.

Chapter 1 laid the foundation by explaining the distinct nature of nonfiction—it's about authenticity, honesty, and emotional resonance. Chapters 2 and 3 guided you in discovering your passion and delving into detailed research, unveiling the raw truth.

Chapters 4 through 6 aided in crafting your narrative, capturing reader attention, and offering them a memorable experience. They're about enabling readers to perceive, feel, and ponder in unprecedented ways. Chapter 7 showed how to convincingly present your viewpoint.

Chapters 8 to 11 navigated you through the finer aspects of enhancing your writing, emphasizing the use of research and stylistic elements. Chapter 12 helped with the fine-tuning of your work, preparing it for the public. Chapter 13 focused on character creation, making them authentic and relatable to readers.

Chapter 14 instructed on how to construct a satisfying conclusion that leaves a lasting impact. Chapter 15 exposed you to methods of publicizing your work, reaching the audience who could benefit most from your writing.

This journey goes beyond writing; it's about establishing a connection, creating an impact, and leaving an indelible imprint. So, use the knowledge you've collected, and create a piece that's truthful, impactful, and representative of your unique voice.

Remember, writing is more than a skill—it's a means of touching people's hearts. It's about communicating something genuine, something significant. You now have the tools for this task. The reins are in your hands now, and you undoubtedly have the aptitude for it. Make it authentic, make it truthful, and make it uniquely yours. Happy writing!

∿

ABOUT THE AUTHOR

Rae A. Stonehouse is a Canadian born author & speaker.

His professional career as a Registered Nurse working predominantly in psychiatry / mental health, spanned four decades.

Rae has embraced the principal of CANI (Constant and Never-ending Improvement) as promoted by thought leaders such as Tony Robbins and brings that philosophy to each of his publications and presentations.

He has dedicated the latter segment of his journey through life to overcoming his personal inhibitions. As a 25+ year member of Toastmasters International he has systematically built his self-confidence and communicating ability. He is passionate about sharing his lessons with his readers and listeners.

His publications thus far are of the personal & professional development, self-help, self-improvement genre and systematically offer valuable sage advice on a specific topic. His writing style can be described as being conversational.

As an author Rae strives to have a one-to-one conversation with each of his readers, very much like having your own personal self-development coach.

Rae is known for having a wry sense of humor that features in his publications. To learn more about Rae A. Stonehouse, visit the Wonderful World of Rae Stonehouse at https://raestonehouse.com.

ALSO, BY RAE A. STONEHOUSE

You may be interested in *The Successful Self-Publisher Series:*

Book One: Writing & Publishing as a Business

Self-publishing can be frustrating to learn, but author Rae A. Stone-house's *Successful Self-Publisher Series* offers advice on writing, publishing, and marketing your own book. The series covers topics such as organizing your content, formatting your manuscript, and creating book titles that sell.

Book Two: Self-Publishing for Fun and Profit

The Successful Self Publisher Series, Book Two: Self-Publishing for Fun and Profit, by author Rae A. Stonehouse, offers advice on self-publishing, covering topics such as proofreading, pricing, royalties, and digital rights management. The book is part of a series that also includes a guide on writing and publishing as a business and one on content marketing strategies.

Book Three Content Marketing Strategies That Work

Writing a book can take up to 30% of your time, while marketing can take up to 130%. However, marketing your content is achievable with basic and advanced strategies, as highlighted in the book "Content Marketing Strategies That Work" by author Rae A. Stonehouse.

All three books are available in e-book, paperback and audio versions. Visit our Live For Excellence online store at https://liveforexcellence. store/product-category/self-publishing/ for more details.

∿

www.ingramcontent.com/pod-product-compliance
Lightning Source LLC
Chambersburg PA
CBHW061147120626
46546CB00005B/1963